FIBONACCI RATIOS

WITH

PATTERN RECOGNITION

Larry Pesavento

TRADERS PRESS®
INCORPORATED
PO BOX 6206
Greenville, SC 29606

*Books and Gifts
for Investors and Traders*

©Copyright 1997 by Larry Pesavento

All rights reserved. No part of this work may be reproduced or transmitted in any form or by any means, electronic or mechanical, including photocopying and recording, or by any information storage or retrieval system without the prior written permission of the copyright owner unless such copying is expressly permitted by federal copyright law.

ISBN 0-934-380-36-8

Published by TRADERS PRESS, INC.

The material contained herein is not to be taken as advice to buy or to sell specific securities. The information presented is based on sources we believe to be reliable and has been carefully checked for completeness and accuracy but cannot be guaranteed.

TRADERS PRESS®
INCORPORATED
PO BOX 6206
Greenville, SC 29606

Books and Gifts
for Investors and Traders

800-927-8222
Fax 864-298-0221
Tradersprs@aol.com

HTTP://Traderspress.com

Table of Contents

1. Preface
2. Introduction
3. Clues from the Cosmos
4. Harmonic and Vibratory Numbers
5. Geometric Characteristics of a Price Chart
6. The Primary Patterns
7. Classical Chart Patterns Using Ratios and Proportion
8. The "Butterfly" Pattern
9. The Opening Price
10. Entry Techniques
11. Appendices
12. Additional Readings

TRADERS PRESS® INCORPORATED
PO BOX 6206
Greenville, SC 29606

Books and Gifts for Investors and Traders

Publishers of:

Commodity Spreads: A Historical Chart Perspective (Dobson)
The Trading Rule That Can Make You Rich* (Dobson)
Viewpoints of a Commodity Trader (Longstreet)
Commodities: A Chart Anthology (Dobson)
Profitable Grain Trading (Ainsworth)
A Complete Guide to Trading Profits (Paris)
Traders Guide to Technical Analysis (Hardy)
The Professional Commodity Trader (Kroll)
Jesse Livermore: Speculator-King (Sarnoff)
Understanding Fibonacci Numbers (Dobson)
Wall Street Ventures & Adventures through Forty Years (Wyckoff)
Winning Market Systems (Appel)
How to Trade in Stocks (Livermore)
Stock Market Trading Systems (Appel & Hitschler)
Study Helps in Point and Figure Technique (Wheelan)
Commodity Spreads: Analysis, Selection and Trading Techniques (Smith)
Comparison of Twelve Technical Trading Systems (Lukac, Brorsen, & Irwin)
Day Trading with Short Term Price Patterns and Opening Range Breakout (Crabel)
Understanding Bollinger Bands (Dobson)
Chart Reading for Professional Traders (Jenkins)
Geometry of Stock Market Profits (Jenkins)

Please write or call for our current catalog describing these and many other books and gifts of interest to investors and traders.

1-800-927-8222   FAX 864-298-0221
Tradersprs@aol.com

HTTP://traderspress.com

*This book
is dedicated to Benida.
You are the reason I am still here to
enjoy all of my friends and family. Everyone
deserves to have someone love them this much in a lifetime.*

PREFACE

Over the past 20 years the use and misuse of the Fibonacci Summation Series proliferated to the point that commentators on the nation's TV business channels now present themselves as resident experts. I lay no claim to being an expert. However, my studies always included an extensive examination of Fibonacci numbers. My pragmatic position on anything I learned is that if I could not use what I was studying to help in trading, then I was not interested in pursuing it any further. If this material stimulates your interest in the subject, then introducing you to it will be worthwhile. A word of caution, this material is based on the probabilities of trading. The art of trading is one of risk management. Amos Hostetter, one of the founders of Commodity Corporation in Princeton, New Jersey, used to say, "*take care of losses and the profits will take care of themselves.*" I refer to this quote a lot because it is very important!

The pattern recognition methodology illustrated in the text will be of interest to anyone who ever traded using technical charts. I can say with confidence there are very few who researched patterns to the extent I have. Some of the references date back to the early 1900's. Each of these patterns is based on ratio and proportion. A technical chart is nothing more than a road map with a price and time axis.

These patterns repeat with a great deal of regularity. My best students have been airline pilots. They seem to approach trading like they approach flying, following a flight plan. The similarities to trading are numerous.

Finally, one of my goals in writing this book is to expose you to the subject of ancient geometry. Fibonacci numbers are an integral part of the numbers that make up the subject of ancient geometry. It will be of interest to some of you that many of these sacred ratios trace their origin to the cosmos. I will not spend a significant amount of time relating my experiences in astro-harmonics research. The subject is too vast for me to consider. More importantly, it is not necessary for profitable trading.

INTRODUCTION

Leonardo de Pisa de Fibonacci and Beyond

On the eastern seaboard about an hour's drive from Florence, Italy lies the town of Pisa. It was here that Fibonacci was born. He was a thirteenth century mathematician who primarily worked for the royal families of Italy. The work for which he is most famous is the *Libre Abaci* (Book of Calculations). His award for this work was the present day equivalent of the Nobel Peace Prize. Fibonacci was largely responsible for the use of arithmetic numbers versus Roman numerals. Before Fibonacci, the number 30 was written XXX. After his *Libre Abaci,* it was written 30.

Legend describes his journey to Egypt as one of great discoveries. He went to Egypt to study the mathematical relationships contained in the pyramids.

Those of you who really want to study the math contained in the pyramids should read Peter Thompkin's book *The Secret of the Great Pyramids*. It is not my intention to explore all of the geometry in the pyramids, only the Fibonacci Summation series. Fibonacci found this series when he studied the Great Pyramid at Giza. The series is the sum of the two previous numbers 0, 1, 1, 2, 3, 5, 8, 13, 21, 34, 55, 89, 144 to infinity. Dividing one number by the next after the eighth sequence yields 21/34 = .618. This just happens to be the relationship of the height of the Great Pyramid to ½ its base. This additive series of numbers is based on the equation

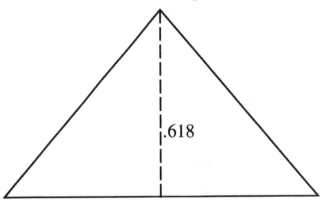

Phi + 1 = Phi squared
(Ø + 1 = Ø²).
Base = 2.00
Half Base = 1.00
Height = .618
Slope = 1.618

Diagonal = 1.902 $\sqrt{(2.618 + 1)}$

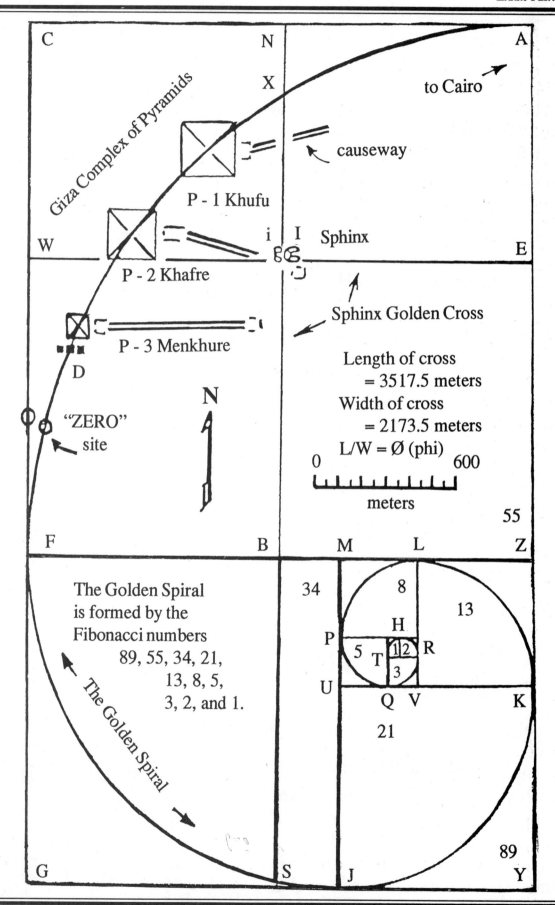

What Fibonacci did for me was to open my eyes! These are the relationships that are constantly in the market. I first started using Fibonacci numbers in 1974 at the urging of John Hill, Sr. of the Commodity Research Institute of Hendersonville North Carolina. I read all of Elliott's papers and his correspondence with Charles Collins. Years later, Frost and Prechter wrote the book *Elliott Wave Theory,* which explained the wave structure and the use of Fibonacci numbers. It concerned me that not all the waves were .382, .500, .618, 1.618. It was not until 1988 that I began using the square root numbers of the Fibonacci series $\sqrt{.618}$ = .786 and $\sqrt{1.618}$ = 1.27. Armed with these two square root relationships, the wave structure can be more easily explained. Bryce Gilmore's first book, *Geometry of Markets* brought the ratios to the public's attention. *The Elliott Wave Newsletter* never used these ratios. I used to fax information to them on the square root numbers, but they never responded. Robert Miner of the Dynamic Traders Group in Tucson, Arizona, uses all of the harmonic ratios. It is my opinion that his newsletter and technical work is the best in our business. If you don't have the time to do the work, Robert Miner, one of the best technicians on this planet, will do it for you at a small monthly cost. This reminds me of one of my favorite quotes from my friend and fellow trader, Jim Twentyman *"Defy Human Nature--Do the work yourself."*

What this book is going to do is illustrate how to use the Fibonacci ratios, their square roots, and their reciprocals to determine the structure of wave vibrations. Of all the books I have in my library, none of the Elliott Wave material covers this important concept. I am going to keep it as simple as possible. If you can glean only one or two concepts or patterns, then this material will not have been written in vain. I can promise you this much. If you study the ratios and patterns shown here, you will realize that markets have a definite pattern hidden within their chaos. Sorting through this chaos can enlighten you. The goal here is not to try to predict the future or even to know what is going to happen next. No one knows that! (Well, there is One who knows, but He doesn't trade.) It is not necessary to know what is going to happen in 5 days. What is necessary is to determine how much risk and profit potential is available in the next 5 days. Probability is the name of the game. Risk control is of tantamount importance. Winners think in terms of how much they can lose. Losers focus on how much they can win. *"Take care of your losses and the profits will take care of themselves."* ---A.B.H.

By end of the book, I hope you see the correlation of geometric patterns to the ratios and proportions illustrated. It is going to be as simple as I can make it for you. Should you want more elaborate reading material it will be listed in the bibliography.

The material here has proved exciting to me and my fellow traders who also subscribe to this approach to the market. In my opinion, it answers the question *"can there be order in the chaos of the market?"* I wish I had known this much about the market 20 years ago!

One more thought about the square root number from the golden mean. These numbers were first revealed in William Garrett's incredible book *The Torque Analysis of Stock Market Cycles*. This is hands down the best book on cycles I ever read. There were only 200 copies sold in 1972. The remainder were destroyed by Prentice Hall due to lack of interest. The book has recently been republished by Ruff Publishing (509-448-6739). An excellent choice for every library.

There are a lot of charts in this book. I know of no other way to illustrate these concepts. Charts were selected from all areas, from commodities to the Dow Jones stocks. Several different time frames were selected because these patterns are found in all time frames.

Do not be disappointed if you do not see the traditional Elliott Wave pattern labeling. It is not neccesary when you use short term pattern recognition. What is important is the ratio and proportion of each wave. Frankly, I never felt too comfortable about exactly identifying the precise Elliott Wave count. This was brought to my attention most vividly several years ago at my trading house in Pismo Beach, California.

Bryce Gilmore and Robert Miner were discussing T-Bonds. They both came up with different Elliott Wave counts. They humbly admitted that they were both right! And these are two of the best technicians I have ever met. Bryce introduced the technician to the true geometry of the market, with his software program and book, *Wave Trader*. I count him as one of my very good friends and I will always be indebted to him. Although Elliott Wave devotees may cringe at this thought, you need not be overly concerned with wave labeling, but the square roots and their reciprocals can go a long way to analyze a wave in the true Elliott sense.

Usually, when I write about a subject, I include the works of other authors. I thought about doing this for a long time but decided to leave the matter alone. There are great many technicians all over the world who could and should be mentioned here. There are even more private traders of equal or greater skill that no one ever hears about. It is out of respect for these unknown artists that I will refrain from mentioning names. I would have left someone out anyway and if it would have been a friend of mine---well, you know the feeling!

The material presented here is not to be considered as a trading system. It cannot stand alone. It is an approach to trading the markets. Judgement and discipline are necessary. And if they can be mastered, the trader has the potential for financial freedom. True freeedom can only come with discipline.

A CLUE FROM THE COSMOS

In the summer of 1986, my good friend and mentor, Dr. Ruth Miller sent me a note. The note stated that October soybean oil would go off the board at 14 cents/lb and begin a huge bull market. I posted the note to my trading monitor and forgot about it until October. After October soybean oil went off the board near the exact price she predicted, I gave her a call. She still lived in Indiana and had a soybean and corn farming operation. Her husband was my first soybean hedge account when I was a broker at Drexel Burnham. During our phone conversations, Ruth revealed to me that she had unearthed (pardon the pun) some incredibly accurate cycles. She said that they were based on planetary movements. Her excitement caused me to be on the next plane to Indiana for a two week tutorial that would change my life forever. Two weeks with her is comparable to a parish priest having the same time with the Pope. Here are just some of the things that came out of that two week stunt at her farm.

1. *Astrocycles Newsletter* was formed. It appeared in more than 22 foreign countries and every state in the union. Five of the G7 countries subscribed.

2. Three books on financial astrology were written over the next six years.
   a) *Astro-Cycles - The Traders Viewpoint*
   b) *Planetary Harmonics of Speculative Markets*
   c) *Harmonic Vibrations*

3. One hundred and fifty traders came to Pismo Beach, California to learn what methodology I used. Most of them are still in contact with me.

4. I gave lectures to thousands of traders in the United States and 8 foreign countries.

5. FNN (now CNBC) invited me regularly as a guest to discuss the planetary cycles in the newsletter.

6. The Pesavento Index was developed at Dr. Miller's urging. It is now a daily part of the Commodity Traders Almanac published by Frank Tauscher of Tulsa, Oklahoma

   The index rates each day by the number of planetary cycles occurring exactly on that date. The average is eight cycles per day. When there are three or less, markets have a strong tendency to change trends. The same is true when there are 13 or more.

I studied a great many approaches to the market over the past thirty years and this ary trader W.D. Gann was an avid proponent of astrology, as was Bernard Baruch. Baruch's comment that *"millionaires don't use astrology, but billionaires do,"* always fascinated me. He employed his own full time astrologer/astronomer, Evangeline Adams. What really drew me closer to the subject were some of my earlier readings. Both Albert Einstein and Isaac Newton were both avid astrologers/astronomers. Once, at a very important meeting, Newton was debating the subject with Johann Kepler, the father of modern physics. After a heated exchange Newton remarked *"the difference between us, dear sir, is that it is quite apparent that I have studied the subject matter extensively and you have not!"*

The first cycle Ruth revealed to me was the Venus-Uranus cycle. She knew I had studied Fibonacci extensively and my interest was guaranteed. Venus takes 255 days to circle the earth and pass through the 360° aspects with Uranus. If you divide 255 by 365 the result is approximately .618 of a year. Since this was the golden mean, I became very excited.

Each year there are 12 or more hard aspects of Venus and Uranus. A hard aspect is one of 30° or multiples thereof:

Fortunately, I had stock market data going back to 1896. All I needed to do was get the Venus-Uranus aspects for all the years from 1896 to 1986. Those 90 years gave me more than 1000 samples of the Venus-Uranus aspects. Jim Twentyman, my good friend and fellow trader at Commodity Corporation, helped me with this study under Ruth's watchful eye.

The research on the Venus-Uranus aspect yielded excellent results. It now has more than 100 years of data and the statistics have held up. The accuracy of timing 3 to 8 day moves in the stock market is truly amazing. Stocks seemed to be pulled upward or downward by this cycle into the date of the aspect.

PLANETARY ASPECTS USED IN TRANSITS

Conjunction 0°
Sextile 60°
Square 90°
Trine 120°
Opposition 180°

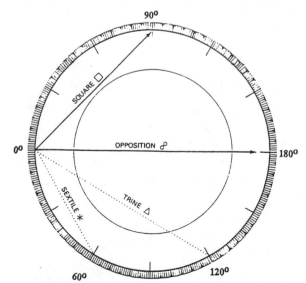

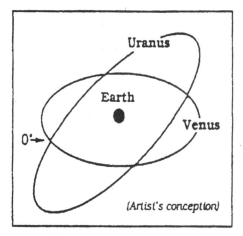

The *Commodity Traders Almanac* lists these aspects as they occur throughout each year.

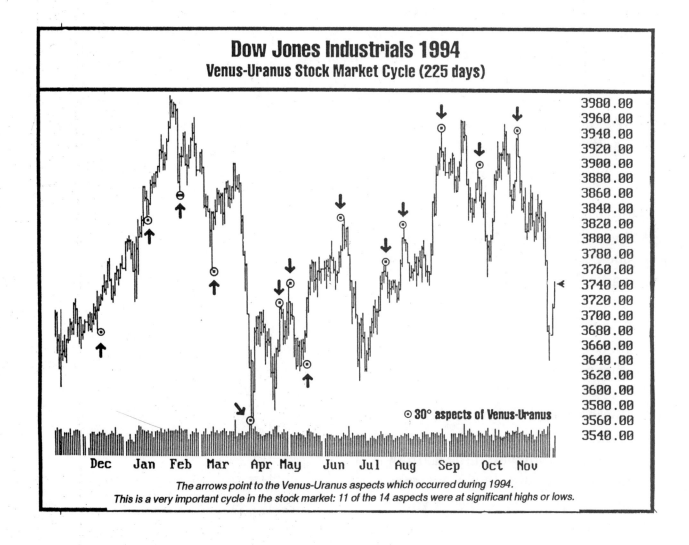

Astrology is a big business throughout the world. Many people plan their lives around it. Most religions banned astrology as a science at the Council of Constantinople in 552 A.D. This is why although Vatican vaults contain the finest astrological material ever written, they are inaccessible to the public. My interest in astrology was purely pragmatic. I was searching for the "*Holy Grail*" of trading. What I did find were several tools that work far above average. But I do believe the markets are vibrating to the tune played by the planets. My reason for this is based on the work of Donald Bradley. Bradley wrote a book *Stock Market Predictions* in 1947. The book was based on forecasting the stock market one year in advance by weighting each of the planets (cycles). Bradley's model is right about 70% of the time in showing the trend of the market for the entire year. This includes some amazing predictions such as the market fall of October 19, 1987, and the big upmove following the attack of Iraq in 1990. The January 1994 stock market surge performed perfectly to the Bradley model. The remarkable part of the model is that it can be completed years in advance and it uses the weighting of the planets as its sole data source. I know of no other technical system that can or will do that.

I know these patterns with ratios and proportion quite well and how their source is in the cosmos. I perform very little astrological research at this time. **These patterns allow you to put probabilities in your favor and control risk easily.** That is what the trader needs at his fingertips.

Harmonic and Vibratory Numbers

I included the section on Harmonic and Vibratory numbers early in this book so the reader will begin to think in terms of repetitions and swings.

Reluctance to share some of their most precious trading secrets is probably inherent in all traders. I am no exception. What you will observe in this chapter is, in my opinion, one of the best kept secrets in technical analysis. These harmonic, or vibratory numbers as I refer to them, can be incredibly useful for profit projection and stop placement. Every commodity, stock, or speculative instrument has its own vibratory number. It is as natural as each element on a chemical chart having its own number. Traders who specialize in trading one speculative vehicle use these numbers all the time. They don't know why, except that they repeat day after day. The next few pages and charts will describe these numbers and illustrate their usage. Make no mistake about this section: it could be one of the most effective tools you can use as a trader.

My first interest in these harmonic or vibratory numbers occurred in 1979 while I was operating the commodity department for Drexel Burnham Lambert in southern California. Jim Twentyman was working with me and occupied the adjoining office. A small window was located between the offices so we could talk without using the phone. Jim had just moved from Conti Commodities where he was a very successful broker/trader. He was now helping me manage my C.T.A. firm, A.V.M. Associates. Jim purchased a Wang computer in 1977 to do research on cycles and numbers. He also took a two year sabbatical to study the works of the legendary trader W.D. Gann.

I had access to the library of the Investment Center Bookstore in West Los Angeles. This library had the finest collection of books I had ever seen. Any book I ever heard about was there, including rare astrological books and old technical books from the 1920s and 1930s. Once you go through this vintage material you will realize there is not a lot that is new to technical analysis. Most assuredly there are new concepts and ideas, but most material can be traced back to earlier traders. I think you will agree that the concept of harmonic or vibratory numbers fits into the "new idea" bracket.

The easiest way to describe why harmonic numbers work the way they do is to use an analogy. Suppose you were to drop a rock into a pool of water. Once the rock hits the water, waves will vibrate from the center of impact until the thrust of the rock hitting the water dissipates. There are four things that will determine the consistency and duration of the waves: 1) The height from which the rock was dropped; 2) The weight of the rock; 3) The depth of the water. (See illustration below.)

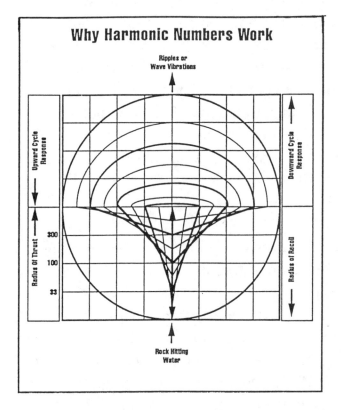

Markets react to thrust in much the same way. Typically, a new announcement or scheduled economic report will cause this thrust in the speculative markets. Currently, the financial markets respond to Gross Domestic Product, employment data, both the Producer Price Index and Consumer Price Index, plus many others. Veteran traders remember vividly how the Money Supply numbers of M^1 and M^2 would shock the markets each week. Now you must search to find these economic numbers. Soon a new leader of economic fundamentals will emerge and the current leaders will take their place in the history books.

Jim Twentyman has an obsession with correct data. He has the best data I have ever seen. It is flawless! What Jim and I did was to categorize all the price swings over a five minute bar chart in all major commodities. The S&P data was done in 1985. We entered each of these into the Wang computer by hand. The computer would then search for values of the price swing and report the frequency distribution of each price swing. When the distribution is skewed you would get a *Poisson* distribution and your first hint of a harmonic or vibratory number. It was then apparent that the only way you could prove this theory was to look at thousands of charts to see if the premise was valid. We tested the idea and found it statistically accurate and quite useful in technical analysis.

Technicians will agree that chart analysis is tantamount to reading a road map. There is an X axis and a Y axis. Chartists depict the X axis for time and the Y axis for price. Once the coordinates are found, you know the exact spot where price and time meet. This information is not going to tell you what will happen next. Nothing can do that! What it does tell you is that a pattern may be completed at that time. The neural network I am using does just that; and harmonic numbers help with this estimation. It has categorized these patterns in time and price. As a trader, I must decide when to enter and exit the market. This is what trading is all about. I then ask myself two questions: 1) Is the pattern and ratio signal present? and 2) Can I afford to take the risk? If the answer to both of these questions is "yes," then I must take the trade. No one

No one can tell which trades will be successful. This is a game of probabilities, but the odds and payoffs are on my side.

The only way you can use harmonic numbers is to go through example after example yourself and see how they work. It is not necessary to know why they work—they just work! Revealing something as important as those numbers used to be of concern to me. Jim Twentyman put my mind at ease with this original quote: *"Defy human nature—do the work yourself!"* That sums it up! Most traders want the work done for them. Is it laziness, lack of commitment or desire? I really don't know. What I do know is that only 10-15 percent of those reading this book will actually go forward and study intraday charts to prove the value of Harmonic Numbers.

The harmonic numbers illustrated here are ones I am sure work. {There is a big clue on how to find vibratory numbers if you are interested and I'll give you that clue at the end of this chapter.}

Order from chaos in the Fibonacci Summation series?

I found it helpful over the years to view any market as a vibration from some energy point. What happened leaves clues to the future of price movements. The Fibonacci Summation Series is related to chaos theory. Within the chaos of market action are identifiable patterns that repeat with great frequency. One of the unusual properties of the Fibonacci series can be illustrated by the following example: take any two numbers from 1 to infinity. Any two numbers will work, but I will start with 124 and 963. Notice what happens when you do the following: add the sum of

```
         124
        +963
  1.    1087
        +963
  2.    2050
       +1087
  3.    3137
       +2050
  4.    5187
       +3137
  5.    8324
       +5187
  6.   13,511
       +8324
  7.   21,835
      +13,511
  8.   35,346
```

When you divide the seventh harmonic vibration by the eighth harmonic vibration you get the number = .618

$$\frac{21,835}{35,346} = .618$$

Once the eighth harmonic is reached there will be virtually no change in the ratio of the numbers as you approach infinity. This is a good example of how two random numbers can be related in the future. Price and time patterns show the same characteristics when they repeat.

S&P   The S&P 500 has a total of five harmonic numbers---three primary and two secondary numbers. Secondary harmonic numbers are important in strongly trending markets. Primary harmonic numbers are: 270, 350, 540. Secondary harmonic numbers are: 170, 110.

Treasury Bonds   Treasury Bonds have a harmonic number of 20. When Treasury Bonds exceed 20 ticks they will most often proceed to 40 ticks. In strongly trending markets multiples of the tick harmonic should be expected (i.e., 2 x 20, 3 x 20, 4 x 20).

Silver   The harmonic numbers for Silver are 18 cents and 36 cents. The second harmonic is 12 cents.

Wheat   The harmonic numbers in Wheat are 17 cents and 11 cents. Multiples of 17 and 11 will appear in strongly trending markets.

Soybeans   The harmonic numbers in Soybeans are 18 cents and 36 cents.

Gold   The harmonic numbers in Gold are $17 and $11.

Swiss Franc and Deutschemark   The harmonic numbers for the Swiss Franc and Deutschemark are 27 and 54 points. The Swiss Franc has a secondary harmonic number of 81 points (27 + 54).

Crude Oil   The harmonic numbers for Crude Oil are 44 and 88 points.

Dow Jones Industrials   The Dow Jones Industrials have a total of three harmonic numbers: two primary (35 and 105) and one secondary (70).

Fibonacci Ratios with Pattern Recognition

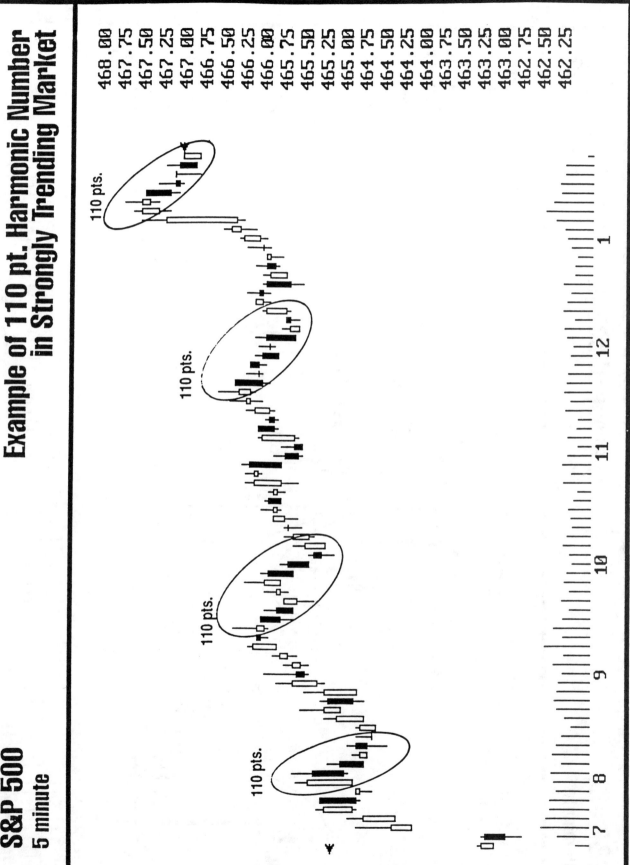

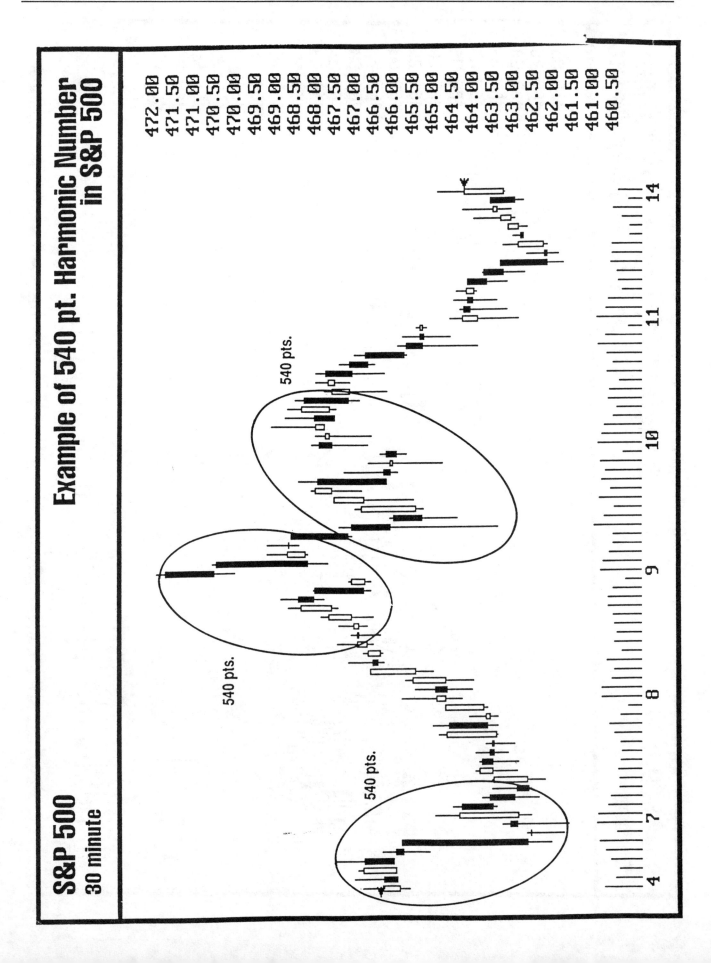

Fibonacci Ratios with Pattern Recognition

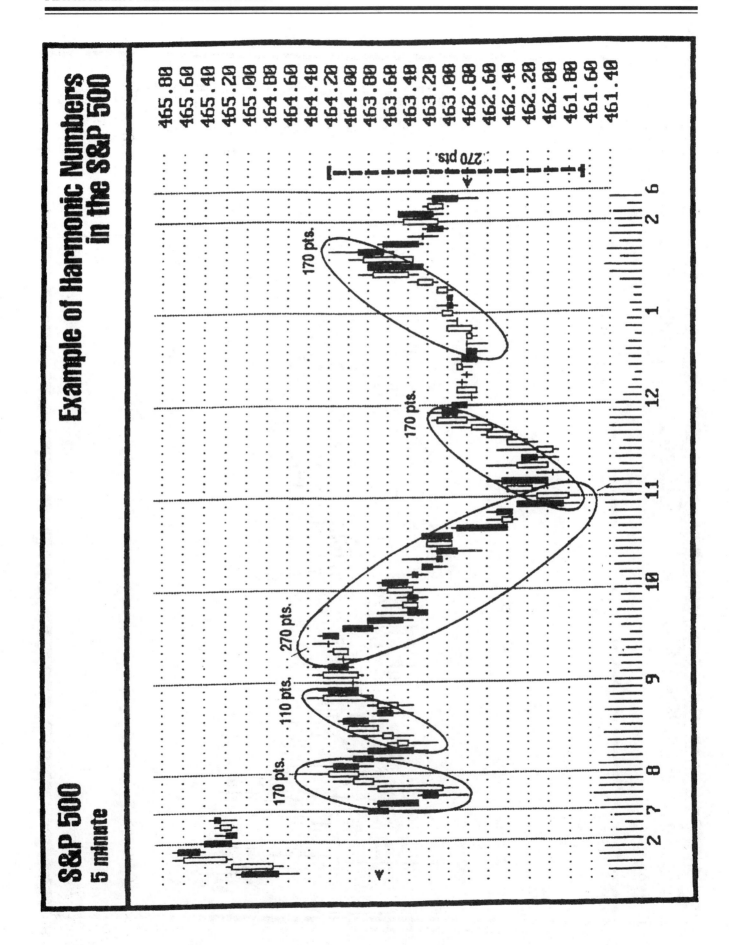

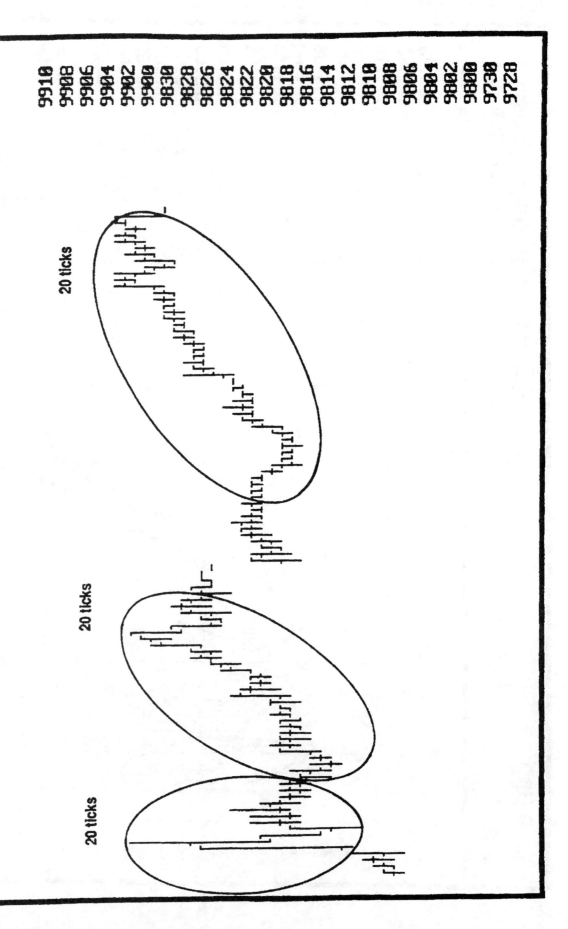

Example of 350 Point Harmonic Number

December S&P 500
5 minute

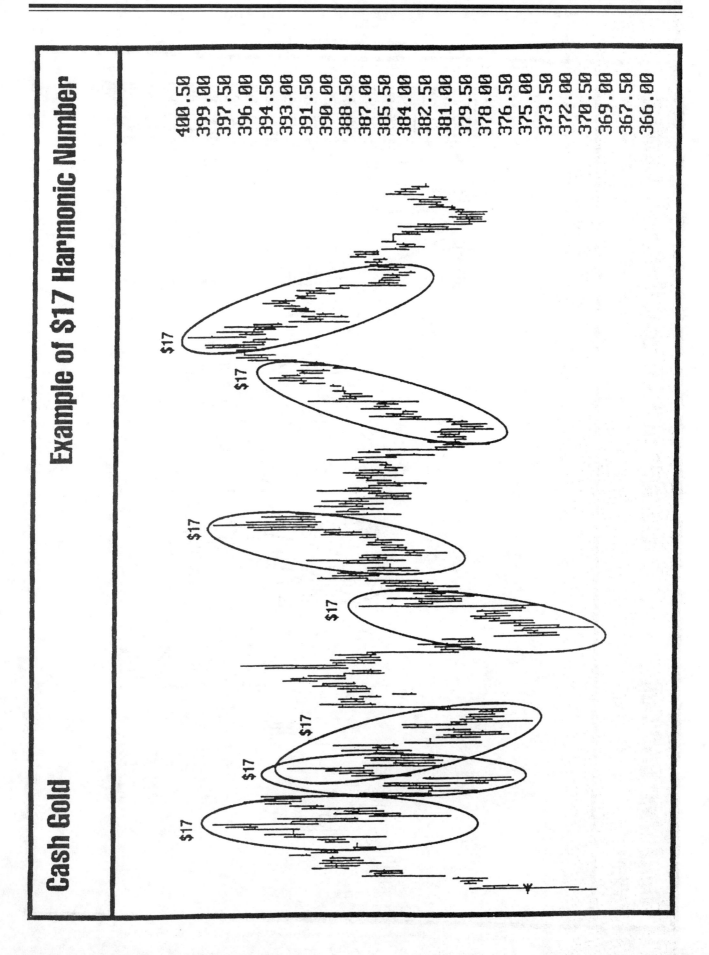

Example of 27 Tick Harmonic Number

December Swiss Franc
2 minute

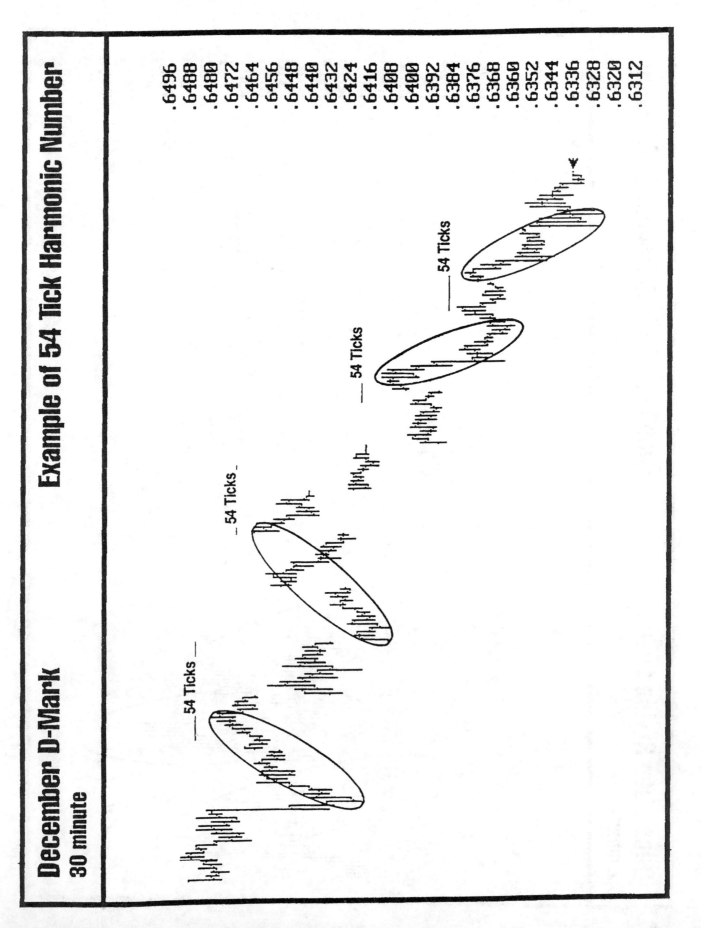

Example of 88 Tick Harmonic Number in Crude Oil

Crude Oil
30 minute

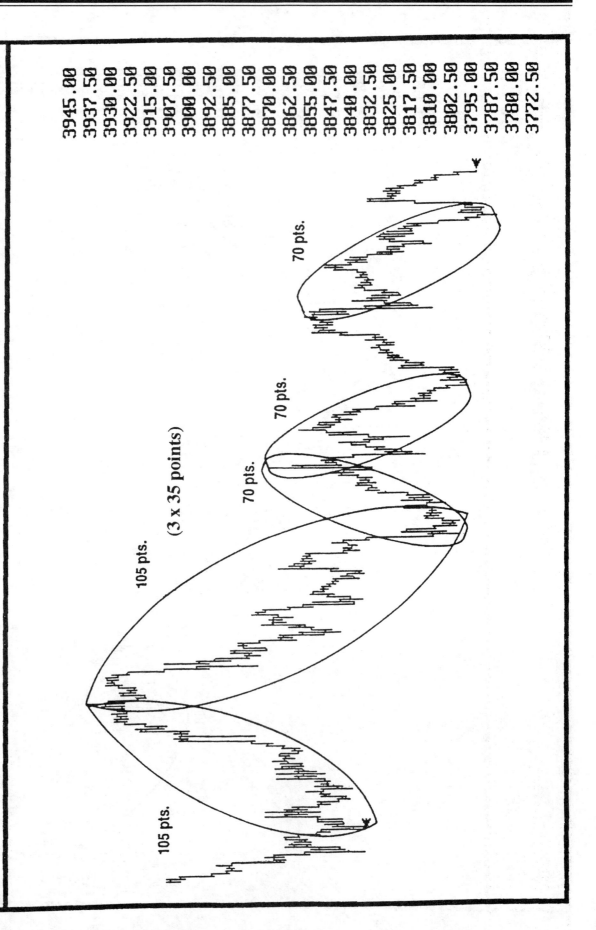

PROPORTIONS OF IMPORTANCE
(Sacred Ratios from 1-5)

RATIO	SOURCE	RECIPROCAL
1.000	$= \sqrt{1}$	= 1.000
1.272	$= \sqrt{1.618}$	= 0.786
1.4142	$= \sqrt{2}$	= 0.707
1.618	$= \phi$	= 0.618
1.732	$= \sqrt{3}$	= 0.577
2.000	$= \sqrt{4}$	= 0.500
2.236	$= \sqrt{5}$ & ϕ $1/\phi$	= 0.447

These ratios are not "sacred" in the religious meaning, but they are sacred to the study of geometry. Just about every price swing imaginable can be found using one of these ratios. For trading the patterns I use, you only need to look for 5 ratios: .618, .786, 1.00, 1.27, and 1.618.

It can be very helpful to know the market you are following is vibratory to .707 or 1.414 instead of the .618 or 1.618.

Finding out why the market did not make one of five ratios can be very important in determining what it is going to do next. The following charts are examples of $\sqrt{2}$ and $\frac{1}{\sqrt{2}}$.

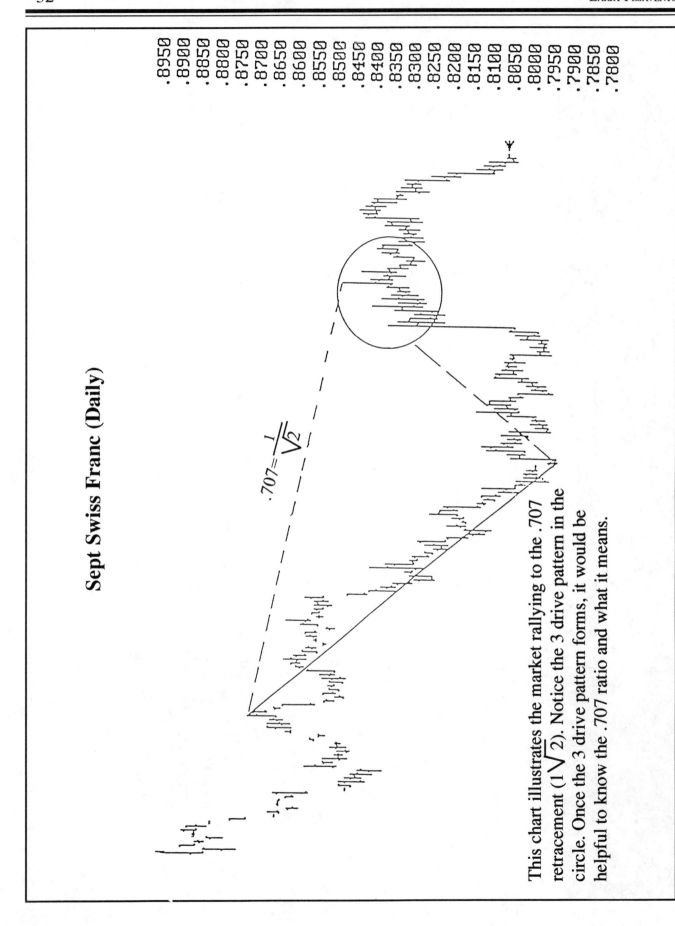

Sept Swiss Franc (Daily)

$.707 = \frac{1}{\sqrt{2}}$

This chart illustrates the market rallying to the .707 retracement ($1\sqrt{2}$). Notice the 3 drive pattern in the circle. Once the 3 drive pattern forms, it would be helpful to know the .707 ratio and what it means.

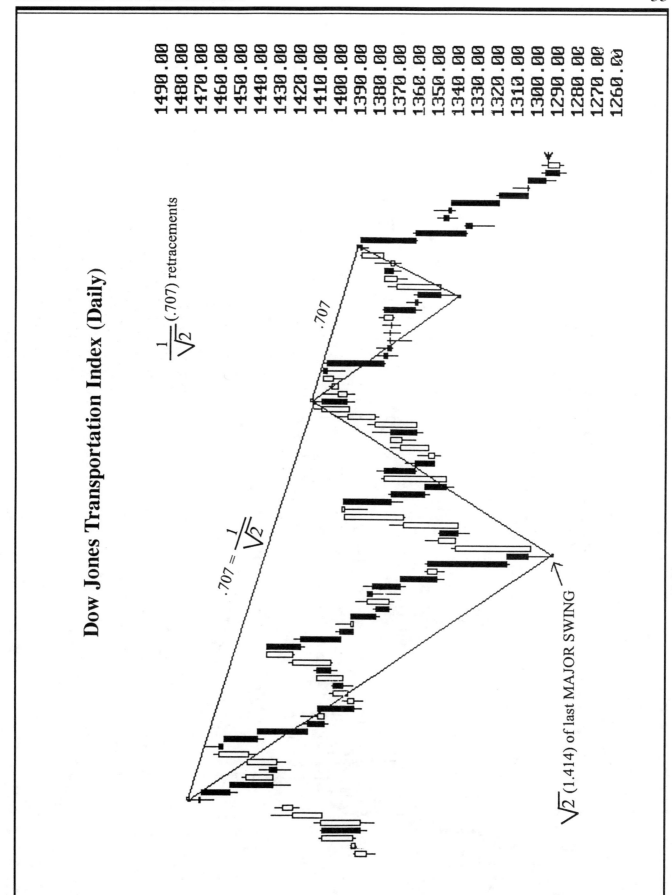

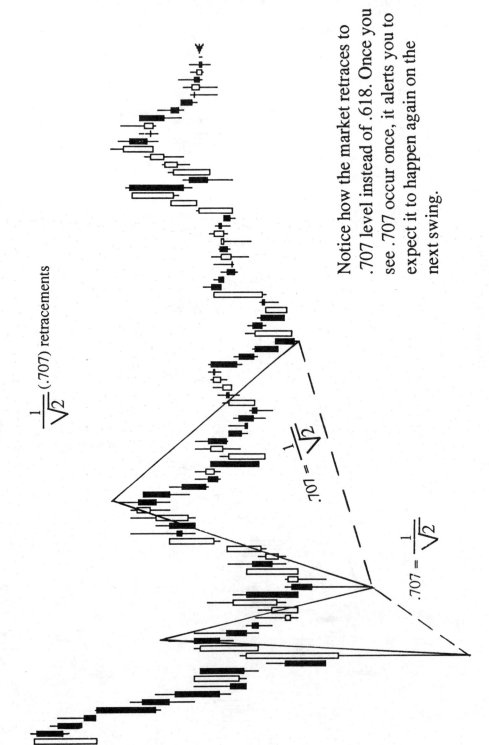

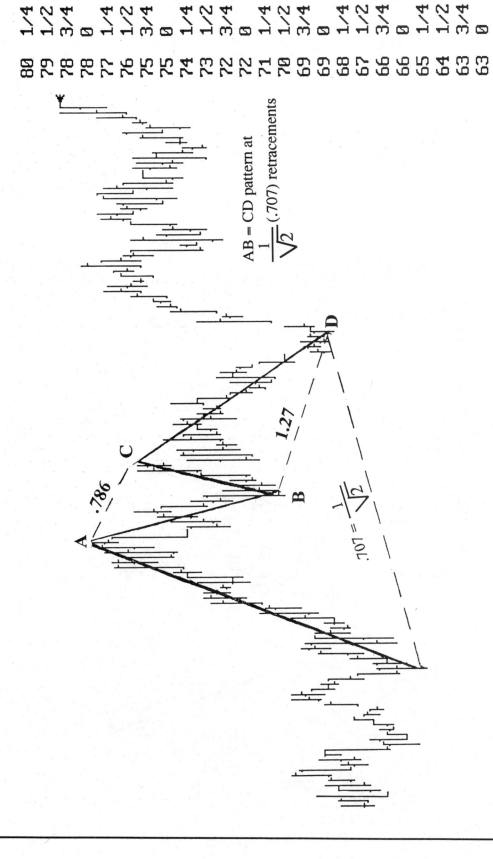

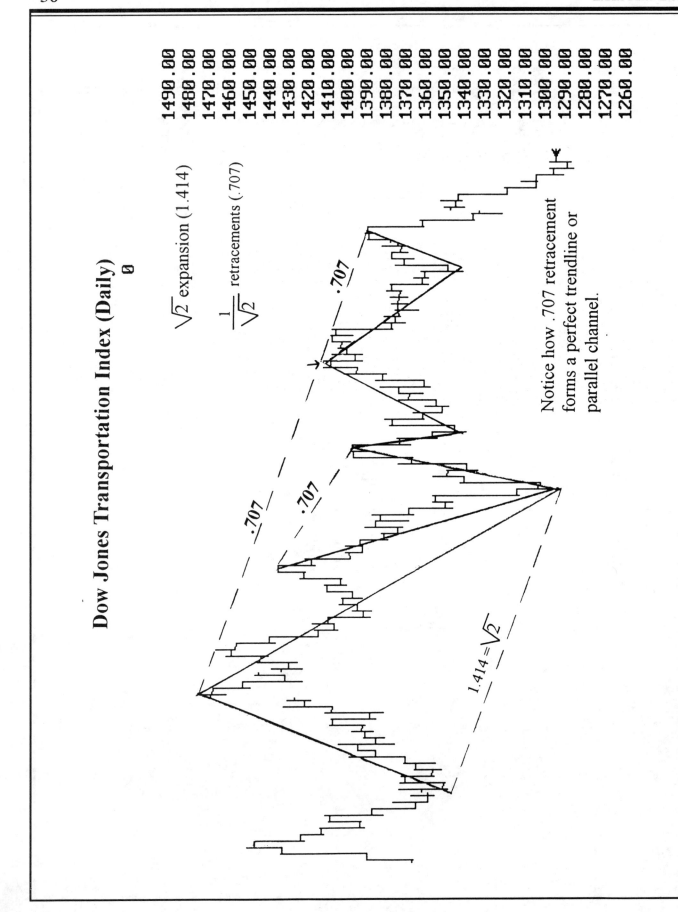

Fibonacci Ratios with Pattern Recognition

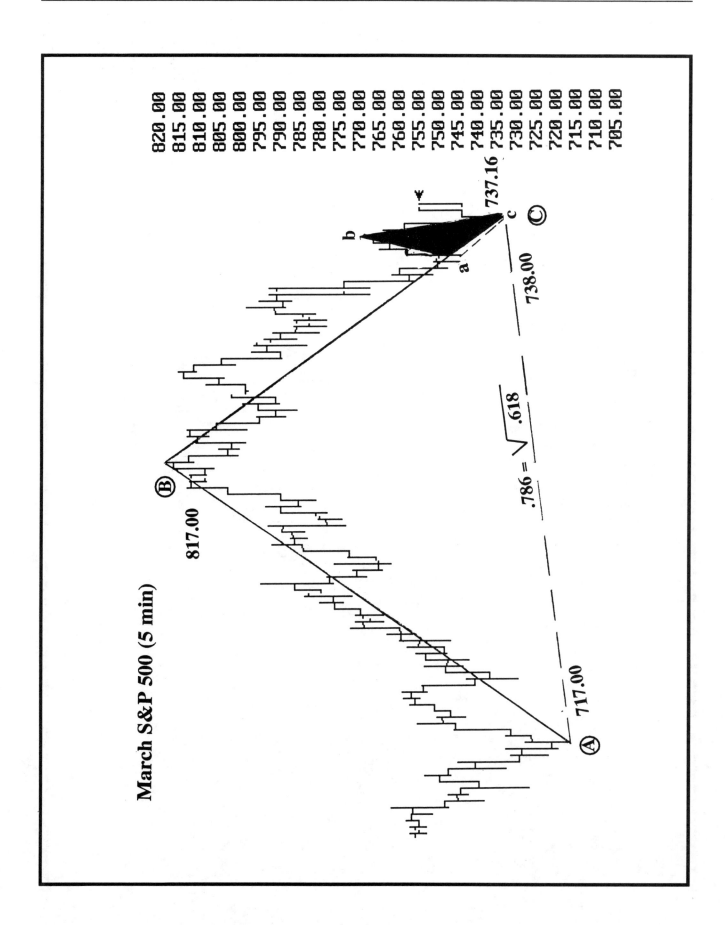

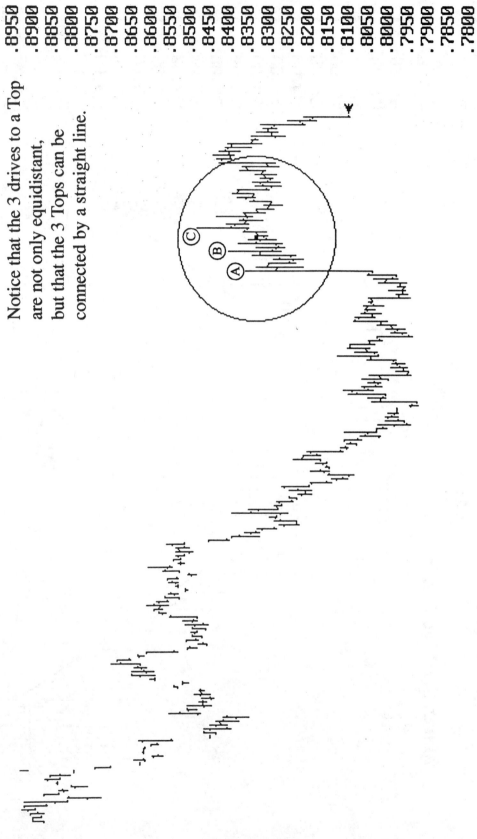

The Geometric Characteristics of a Price Chart

Technicians use price charts to interpret what the next move is most likely to be. Let us consider the following:

A price chart is a square

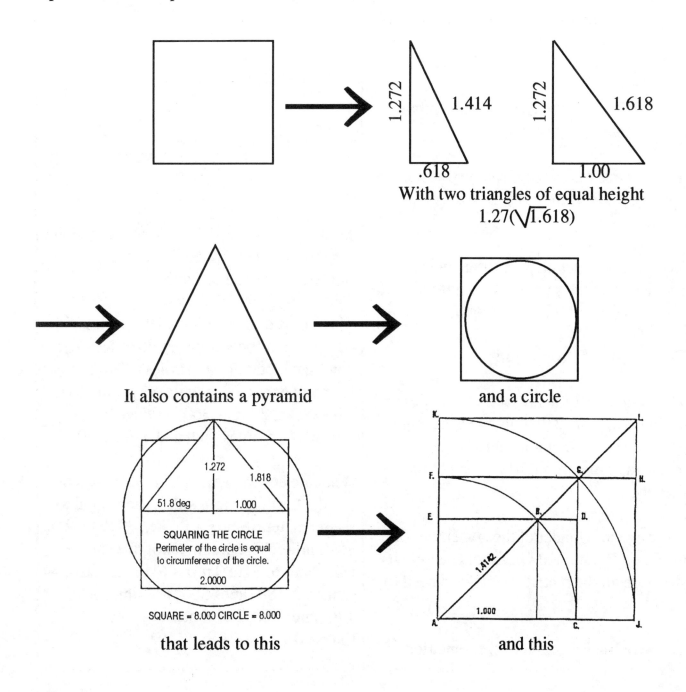

Geometric Principles
(by Bryce Gilmore)

Philosophical Geometry

Ancient philosophers taught pupils the arts of SACRED GEOMETRY in order to develop their faculty of INTUITION.

Geometry attempts to recapture the orderly movement from an infinite formlessness to an endless interconnected array of forms, and in recreating this mysterious passage from ONE to TWO, it renders it symbolically viable.

The practice of Sacred Geometry is one of the essential techniques of self-development.

Geometry deals with pure form, and philosophical geometry reenacts the unfolding of each form out of the preceding one.

The Canon of Proportion

The binding natural law of mathematics as we know it today ORIGINATES from the COSMOS. It was not invented by man, just revealed to him through his study of the Planets.

The Seventh wonder of the ancient world, the Great Pyramid of Giza, holds within its structure all the math "secrets" we need to know.

The pyramid is a graphic representation of the Earth and Moon and their combined movements around the Sun. The pyramid demonstrates the binding relationships between the SQUARE, CIRCLE and the GOLDEN MEAN.

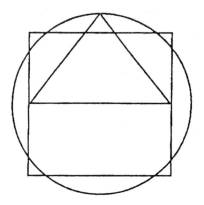

Modern day scientific studies have (among other things) confirmed the measurements of the Moon and the Earth.

The radius of the Moon is 1090 miles and the radius of the Earth is 3960 miles. A combined total of 5040 miles (Plato's mystical number and in calendar days equal to 720 weeks, 2 times 360, 3 times 240, 4 times 180, 5 times 144, and 8 times 90).

A square encompassing a circle representing the Earth has four sides, each equal to the diameter of the Earth, i.e., 3920 by 2 or 7920 miles. The perimeter of this square calculates to 31680 miles (4 times 7920, 44 times 720, 88 times 360, 132 times 240, 176 times 180, 220 times 144, and 352 times 90).

If the Moon and the Earth were placed side by side, the distance between the two centers would be equal to the sum of the radii, i.e., 3920 plus 1080, which equals 5040 miles. A circle drawn using the combined radii of 5040 would have a circumference of 2 Pi R or 2 x 22/7 x 5040, which equals 31680.

The relationship of the circle's circumference to the square's perimeter is 1.000:1.000.

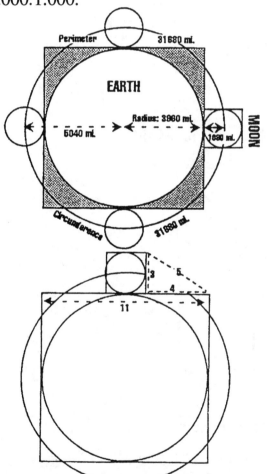

This geometric exercise is known as squaring the circle. Pi is the Pythagorean measure of 22/7 used to calculate the dimensions in a circle or sphere. In decimal form Pi is the irrational number 3.14159.

The radius of the circle 5040 (1080 + 3960) as a factor of the Earth's radius is equal to 5040:3960 or 1.2727:1.000. And 1.272 is mathematically the square root of 1.618.

Squaring the Circle

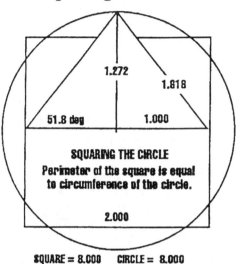

A hypotenuse calculation for a right-angled triangle using the 5040 radius of the above circle and half the side of the above square, i.e., the radius of the Earth 3960, would give the following result.

Using the Pythagorean theorem, i.e., the length of the hypotenuse in a right triangle (90 degree triangle) will be equal to the square root of the sum of the squares of the other two sides.

Hypotenuse = square root [(5040 x 5040) + (3960 x 3960)] = 6409 miles.

If we call the base of the triangle the Earth's radius, i.e., 3960, then the hypotenuse 6409.6 as a ratio of the base 3960 is 6409:3960 or 1.618:1.000.

The irrational number 1.272 is the square root of 1.618, i.e., $1.272 = \sqrt{1.618}$.

It can be demonstrated by this exercise where the designers of the Great Pyramid of Giza procured their measurements. It can also be seen that the irrational numbers of $\emptyset = 1.618$ and $\Pi = 3.14159$ are related.

$$1/4 (3.142) = 0.786 (1/\sqrt{.618})$$

1/4 is the harmonic ratio from the square and 1.618 is the Golden Mean.

Harmonic Ratios from the Square
The Diagonal of the Square
(Root 2 = 1.4142)

The square is bounded by four equal sides at right angles to each other.

Using the Pythagorean theorem we can calculate the diagonal length. This number will always maintain the same relationship to any side of the square (1.4142:1).

A square with sides equal to 1.000 has a diagonal of: $\sqrt{(1^2 + 1^2)}$ or $\sqrt{2}$, which is 1.4142.

The diagonal of any square relates as 1.4142:1.000 with its side.

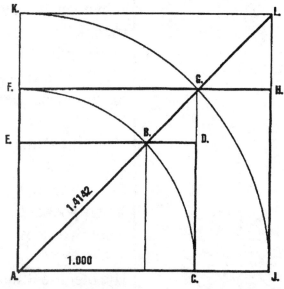

Expanding a square by the ratio of its diagonal produces the Harmonic Ratio Series.

      1.000   1.4142   2.000   2.828

The inverse ratio relationships are:

      0.354   0.500   0.707   1.000

THE PRIMARY PATTERN

This section discusses the primary patterns I use in trading. Many of my students ask me why I share this information. It is quite simple and has a two part answer. First, all of these patterns were found by someone else over the past 70 years. Second, every trader has his own time frame that he likes to trade, so the chance of a self-fulling trade expectation is very remote.

One very important difference will emerge from this section on pattern recognition. That difference is that all of the patterns discussed will be illustrated using the mathematical ratios of ancient geometry, of which the Fibonacci Summation series is a part. What I tried to do is show how you can use only four numbers of the Fibonacci Summation series to mathematically identify these patterns. I always thought that the mathematical relationship of these price swings is what the originators of these patterns failed to bring up. This is especially true for the Elliott Wave theoreticians. I studied the Elliott Wave principle extensively from 1974 to 1978. I thought his tenets on wave patterns were more like guidelines than immutable laws. To this day, if you get 12 Elliott Wave theorists in a room you will end up with 24 or more interpretations of the price action. There is nothing wrong with that. It is just another way of showing that no one knows what is going to happen next in the markets. More importantly it also reiterates that it is not necessary to know what is going to happen next. What is necessary is to **know the risk** on the trade. Since we are dealing with mathematical relationships, the control of risk can be quantified easily.

I spent the better part of 30 years looking at these patterns. My sources originated from Don Mack at the Investment Center in Santa Monica, California and John Hill at the Commodity Research Institute in Hendersonville, North Carolina. I do not think I overlooked anyone who ever described a price pattern. There are two books that I highly recommend:

1. *Profits in the Stock Market* by H.M. Gartley (1935). This was Gartley's Stock Market course in the 1930's. It cost $1500 which was equivalent to 3 Ford automobiles at the time. On pages 200 to 250 most of the patterns ever discussed are found. More trading systems were rediscovered and sold from this book than any other book. This includes: The Tubbs Stock Market Course, The Trident Strategy, The Reversal Point Wave, and many others. The book is more than 700 pages and comes with huge wall charts illustrating the action of the stock market in the 1920's and 30's. It can be purchased for under $100 from Traders Press in Greenville, SC, 800-927-8222.

2. *Torque Analysis of Stock Market Cycles* by William Garrett (1971). This book is a true gem. It was the first book ever written that explores the mathematical and geometrical relationships of price patterns and how they relate to the numbers of ancient geometry. Garrett's book came out at about the same time as another book on cycles. James Hurst's *The Profit Magic of Stock Transaction Timing*. Hurst's book was less expensive and much easier to read. But the content of Garrett's book held the key to many answers about cycles and Fibonacci numbers. Only 200 copies of Garrett's book were ever sold. Prentice Hall destroyed the remainder of copies due to the need for warehouse space.

If you spend some time looking through my bibliography, you will see that a great number of authors are covered. I always felt that each of them contributed to the science of technical studies.

The Ten Basic Patterns

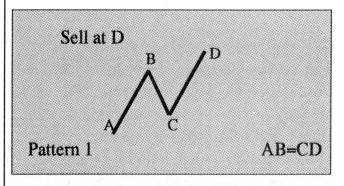

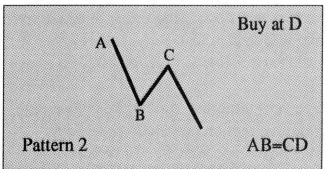

Patterns 1 and 2 were first described by H. M. Gartley in *Profits in the Stock Market* on page 249. It is the basic pattern in the theory of parallel channels.

PRACTICAL USE OF TREND LINES

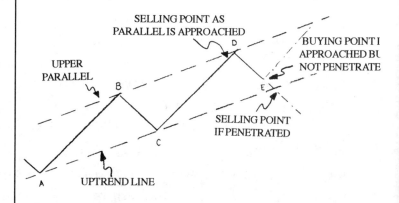

From this one page in Gartley's book, two of the most famous trading systems were sold. The first was the Tubbs Stock Market course ($1500 in the 1950's) and The Trident Strategy ($3000 in 1970's).

The Gartley "222" Pattern

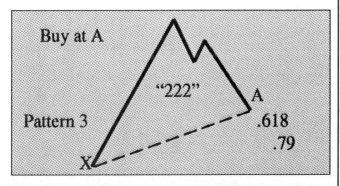

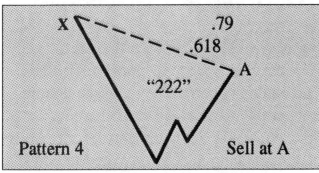

This is one of the best patterns I ever found. I named it the Gartley "222" pattern because it is on page 222 in Gartley's book. He spent more time describing this pattern than all the others. This pattern shows why it is not necessary to pick a top or bottom--- just wait for the first "222" pattern following the top or bottom. The real beauty of this pattern is that it contains an AB=CD pattern within it. This allows the trader to calculate ratio and proportions of various price waves in order to determine the risk on the trade. If the day trader can learn only this pattern he will do very well. It is worth noting that when the "222" pattern fails (market moves beyond point X) a major continuation move is in progress.

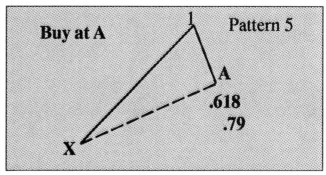

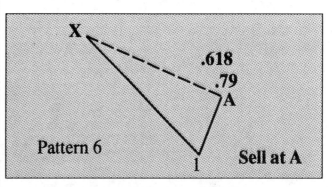

Patterns 5 and 6 are reaction patterns. The move from point 1 can be 38%
          50%
          61%
          70.7%
          78%
          100% (double
               top or
               bottom)

The only time I use the 38% retracement level to find a trade entry is when the move from X to 1 is one of tremendous thrust (3 to 5 times normal trading range bars). The market will give you strong clues as to what it will do next if you watch the retracements in new moves. If it reacts only 38% on the first reaction swing, then a high probability exists that the next swing or two will also be 38% reactions.

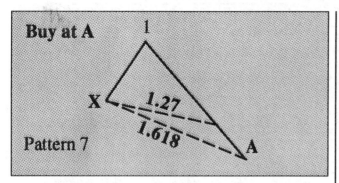

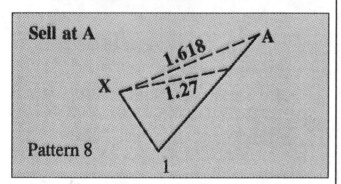

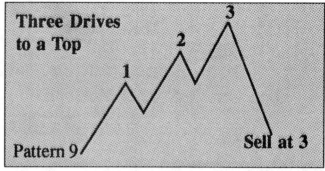

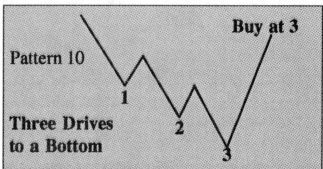

Patterns 7 and 8 are extension patterns. It was this pattern that changed my approach to trading. As I was trading from Switzerland, where I had spoken to a group of Swiss bankers, almost every trade I put on over the last several days had been stopped out on a penetration of point X. In my hotel room, I was calculating why my stop was right at the high/low of the day. I had placed my stop right at the 1.27 move of X to 1. It was upon hitting the square root button on my calculator that I first began to see the importance of the 1.27 ratio $\sqrt{1.618} = 1.27$.

A good rule of thumb is to wait for a candlestick pattern such as a *doji* or *hammer* (pg.118) when point A is reached. Remember that this pattern is an extension pattern and there are no guarantees that the swing cannot go much higher.

Patterns 9 and 10 are the most difficult to find on daily charts. They are found more frequently on intraday charts (5 min., 30 min., etc.). William Dunnigan described this pattern in Dunnigan's One-Way Method and the Dunnigan Thrust Method. The three drive pattern should be very esthetic to the eyes of the trader. It should jump out at you. If you find that you are forcing the pattern to fit three drives, it is probably not correct.

The most important thing to keep in mind is symmetry. The waves should be symmetrical in price and time.

Note: Linda Bradford Raschke refers to this pattern as her *Three Little Indians* in her book, *Street Smarts*.

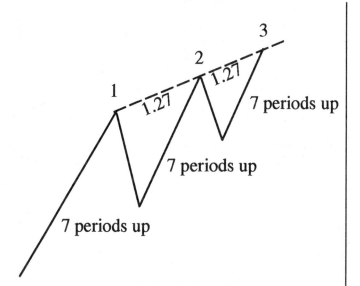

The diagram above is an example only. It shows the number of periods could be 3 to 13. The price swing could also be 1.618.

Characteristics of Patterns

PATTERN #1

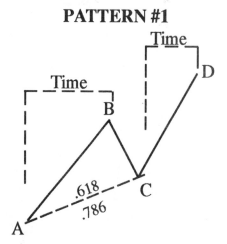

1. Price swing from A to B will be equal to CD 60% of the time. The other 40% of the time CD will be 1.27 or 1.618 of AB.

2. The BC price swing will be .618 or .786 of the AB move. In very strongly trending markets the BC swing will only be at the .382 retracement.

3. If the AB swing is very strong, it will give a good clue as to what to expect on the BC move.

4. The time bars from point A to B should be equal to the CD time bars about 60% of the time. The other 40% of the time these time periods will expand to 1.27 or 1.618 of AB.

5. Should the CD price swing have a price gap or a very wide range bar, the trader should interpret this as a sign of extreme strength and expect to see price expansions of 1.27 or 1.618.

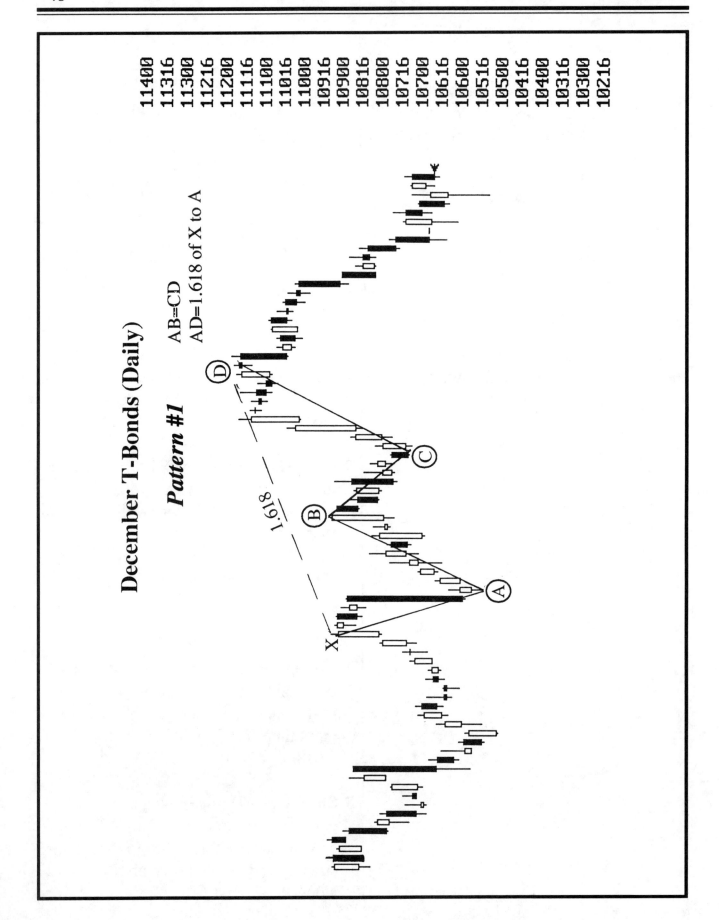

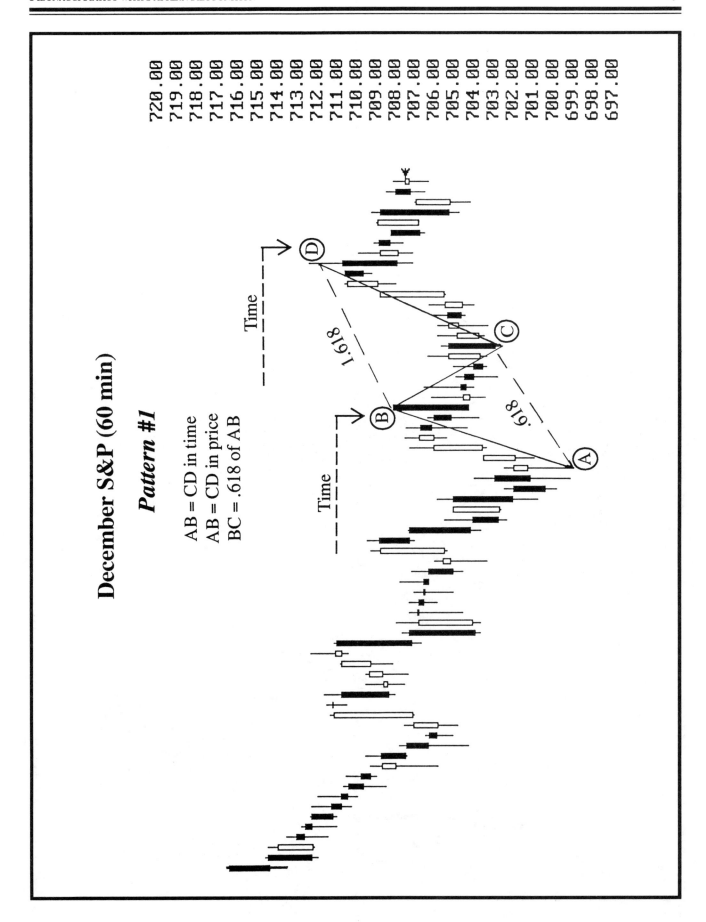

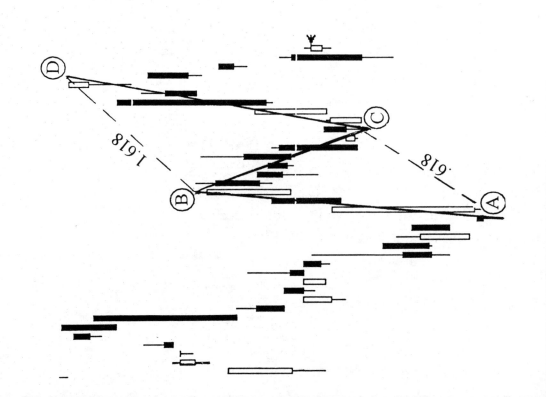

PATTERN #2

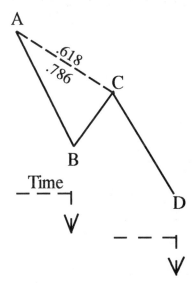

1. Price swing from A to B will be equal to CD 60% of the time. The other 40% of the time CD will be 1.27 or 1.618 of AB.

2. The BC swing will be .618 or .786 of the AB move. In very strongly trending markets the BC swing will only be at the .382 retracement.

3. If the AB swing is very strong, it will give a good clue what to expect on the BC move.

4. The time bars from point A to B should be equal to the CD time bars about 60% of the time. The other 40% of the time these time periods will expand to 1.27 or 1.618 of AB.

5. Should the CD price swing have a price gap or a very wide range bar, the trader should interpret this as a sign of extreme strength and expect to see price expansions of 1.27 or 1.618.

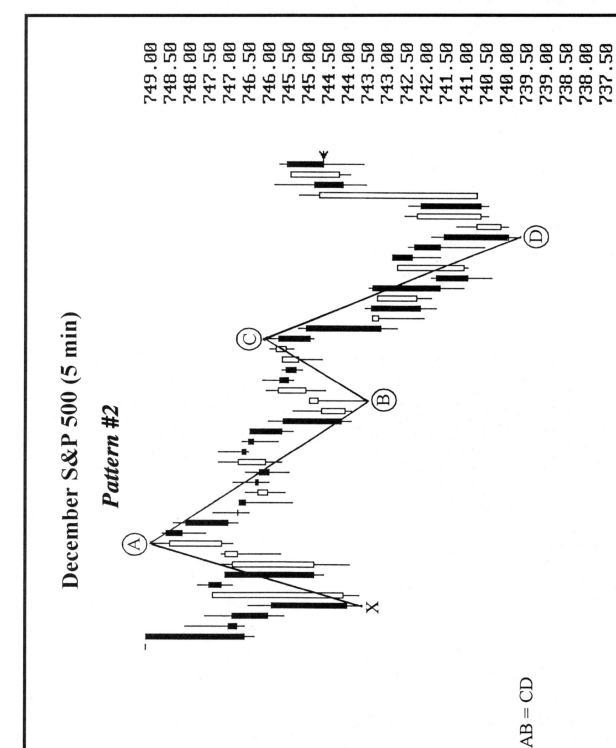

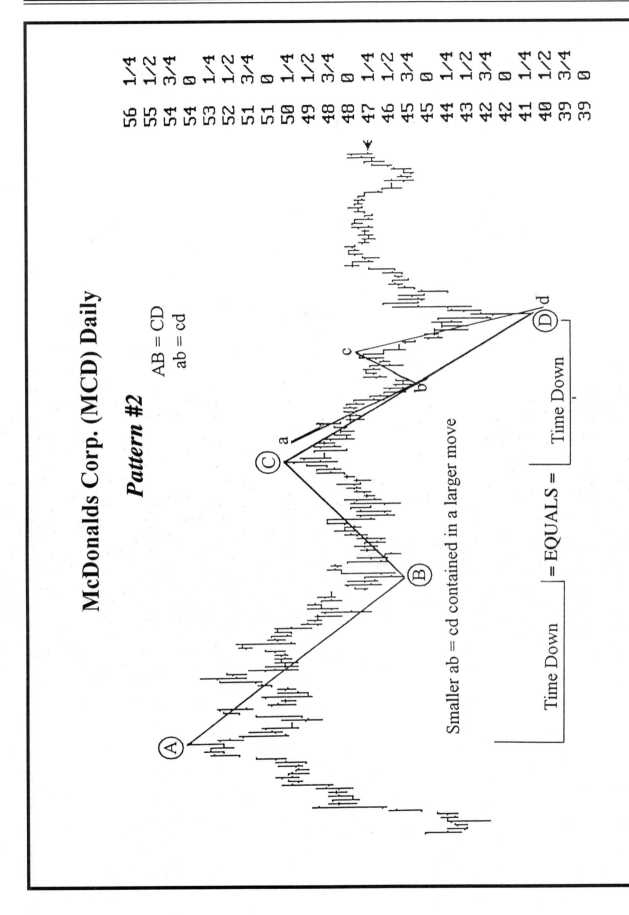

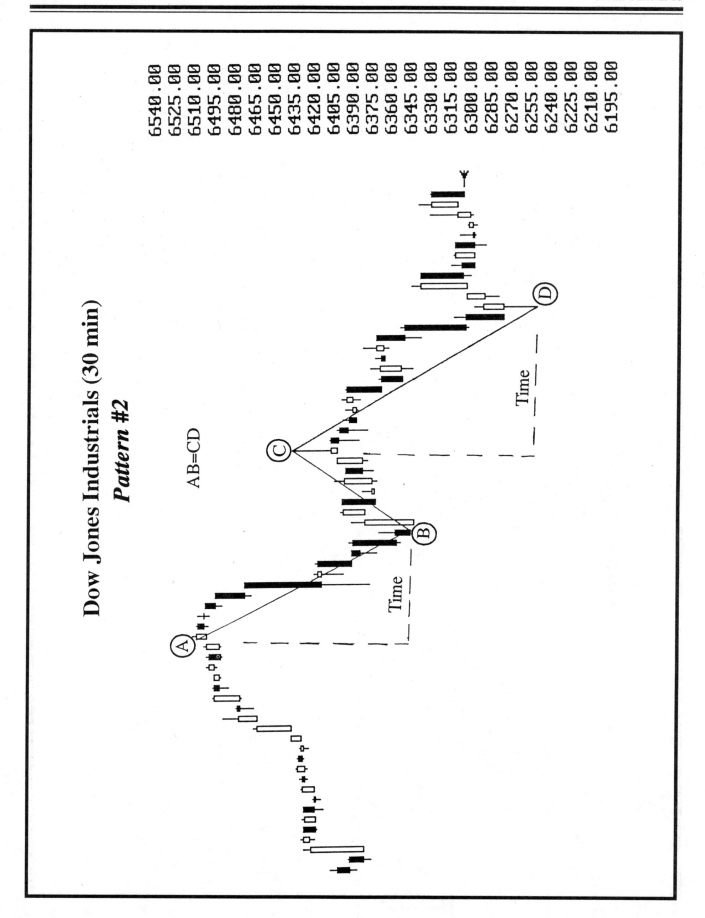

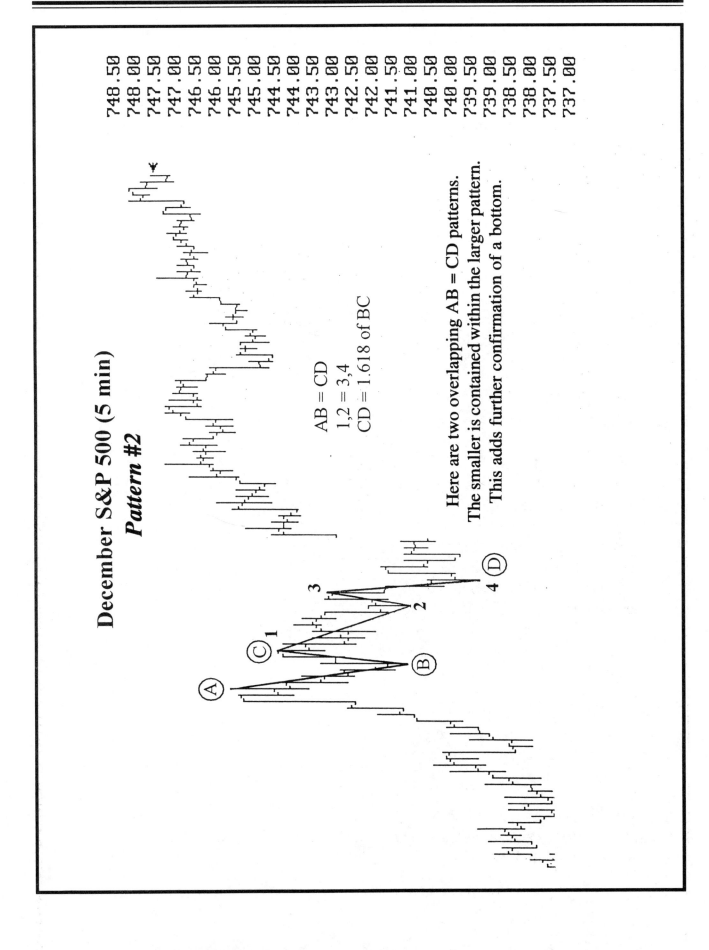

PATTERN #3
BULLISH
GARTLEY "222"

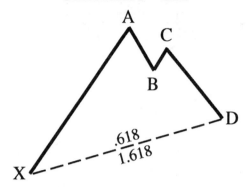

1. The swing down from point A will terminate at point D. This will be at the .618 or .786 retracements 75% of the time. The other 25% of the time, the retracements will be .382, .500 or .707.

2. There must be an AB = CD pattern observed in the move from A to D.

3. The BC move will be .618 or .786 of AB. In strongly trending markets expect a .382 or .500 retracement.

4. Analyze the time frames from point X to A and A to D. These time frames will also be in ratio and proportion. For example, the number of time bars up from point X to A is equal to 17 bars. The time bars from A to D equal 11. Seventeen is approximately 1.618 of 11.

5. There will be a few instances where the AB = CD move will give a price objective at point X. This will be a true double bottom formation.

6. If point X is exceeded the trend will continue to move down to at least 1.27 or 1.618 of the X to A move.

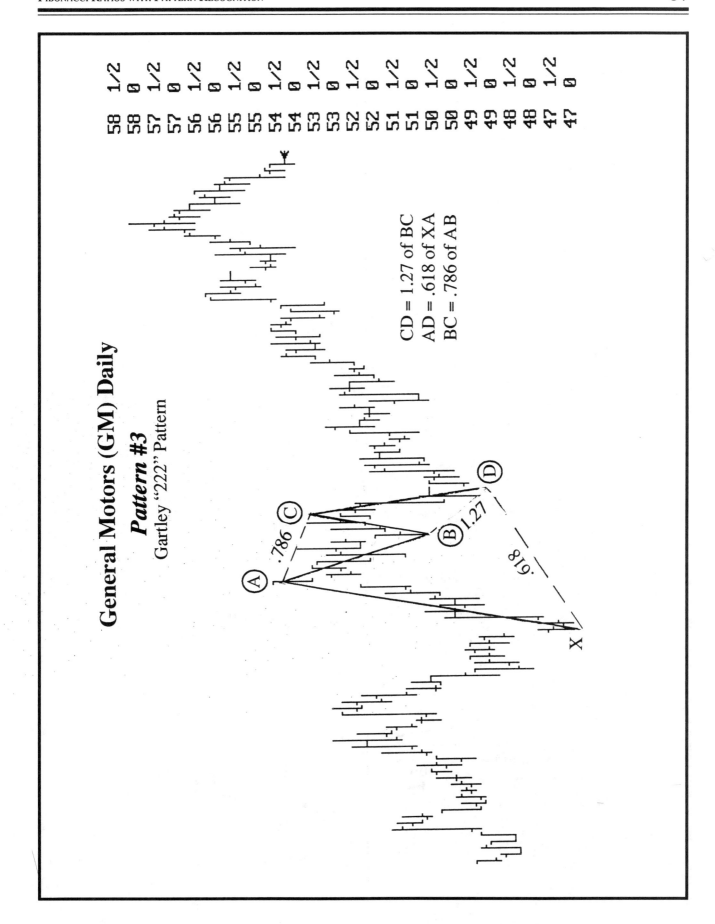

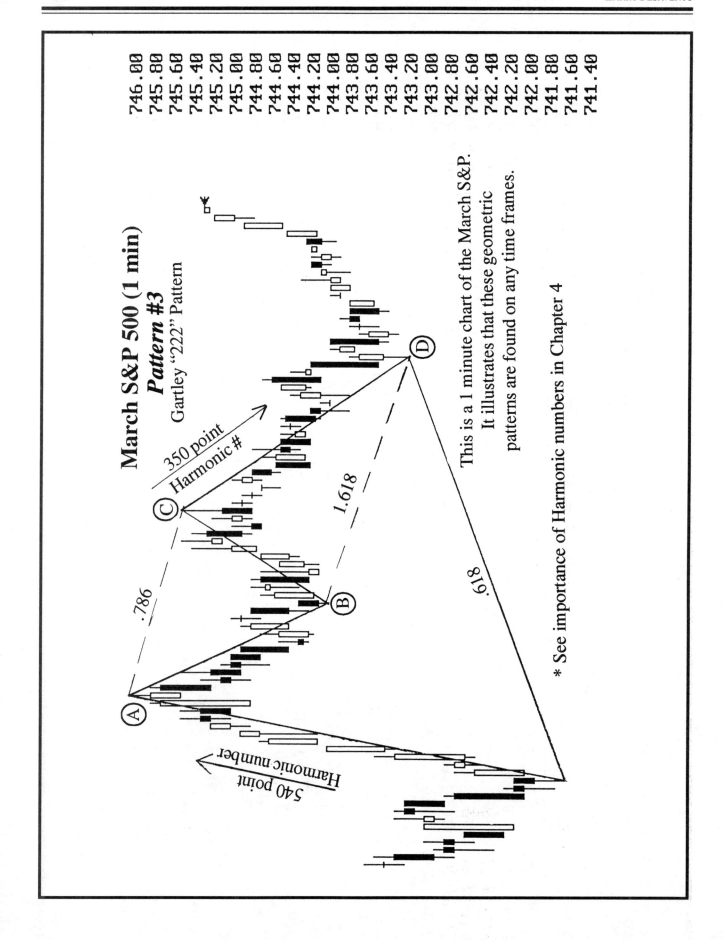

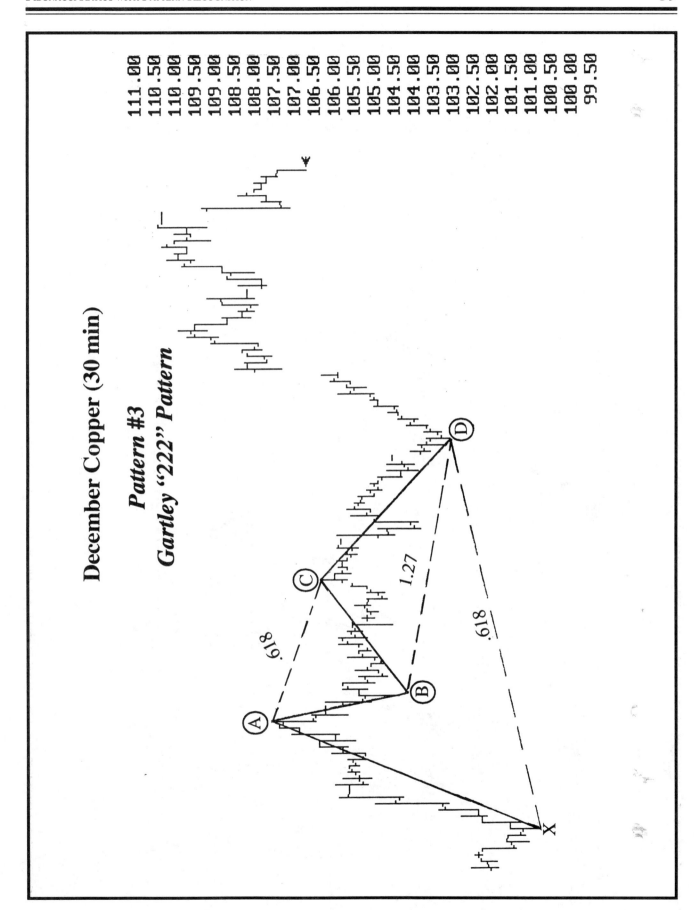

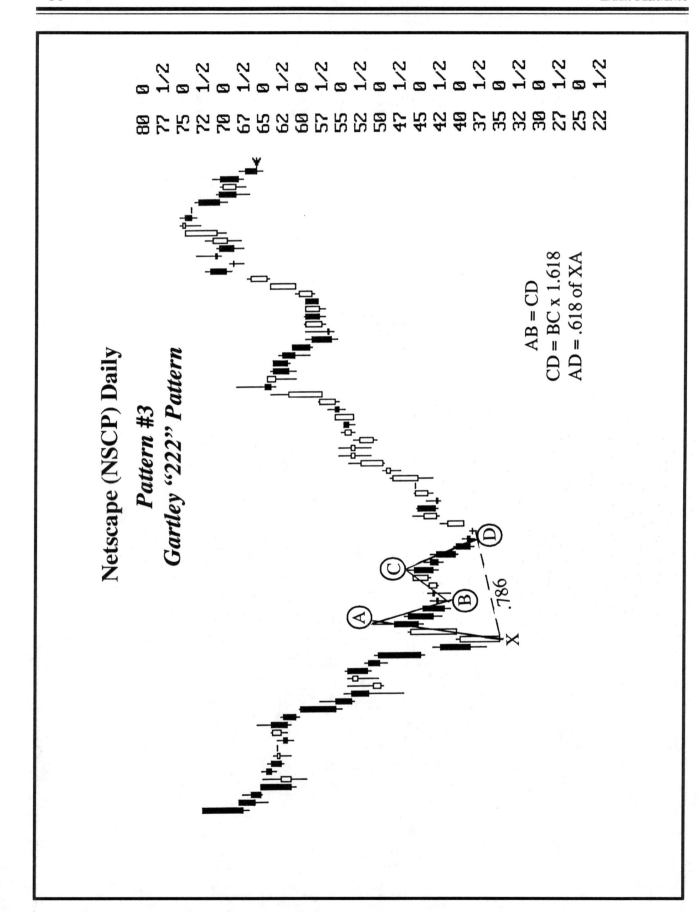

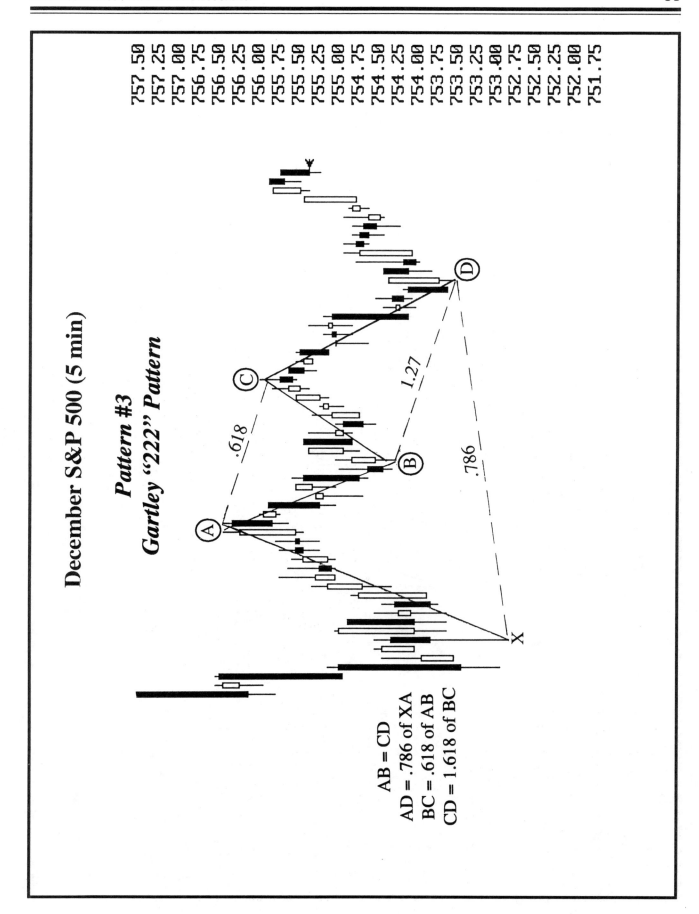

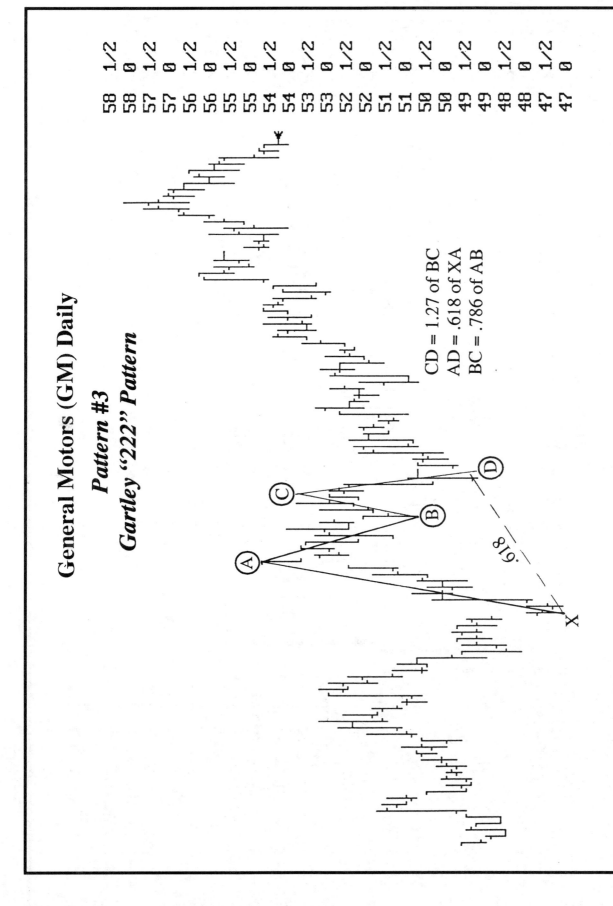

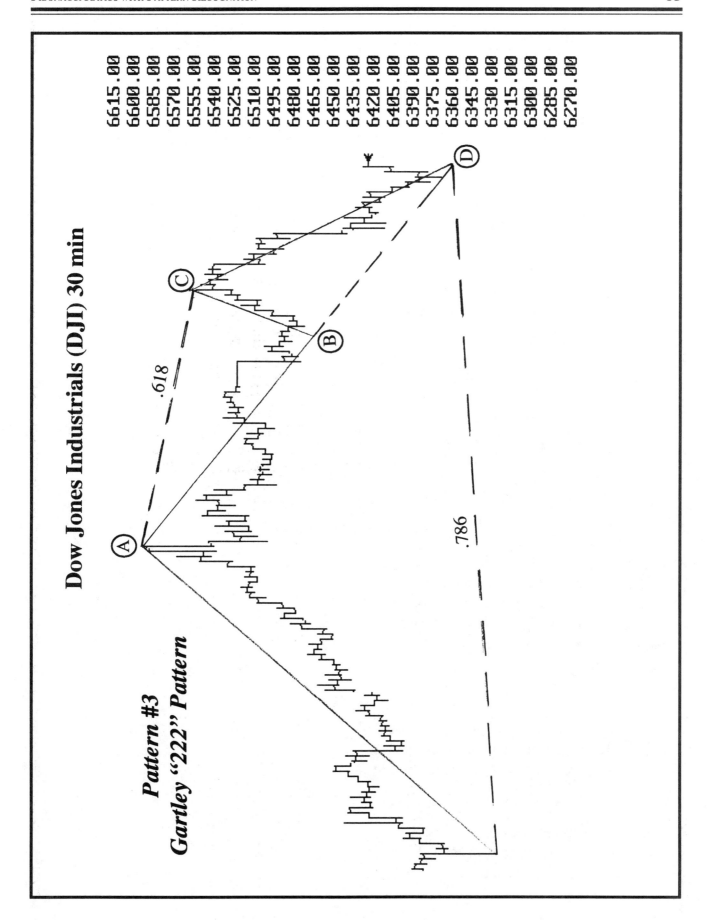

PATTERN #4
BEARISH
GARTLEY "222"

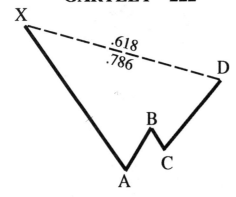

1. The swing up from point A will terminate at point D. This will be at the .618 or .786 retracements 75% of the time. The other 25% of the time, the retracements will be .382, .500 or .707.

2. There must be an AB = CD pattern observed in the move from A to D.

3. The BC move will be .618 or .786 of AB. In strongly trending markets expect a .382 or .500 retracement.

4. Analyze the time frames from point X to A and A to D. These time frames will also be in ratio and proportion. For example, the number of time bars down from point X to A is equal to 17 bars. The number of bars from A to D is 11.

5. There will be a few instances where the AB = CD move will give a price objective at point X. This will be a true double top formation.

6. If point X is exceeded the trend will continue to move up to at least 1.27 or 1.618 of the X to A move.

General Telephone & Electric (GTE)

Pattern #4
Gartley "222" Pattern

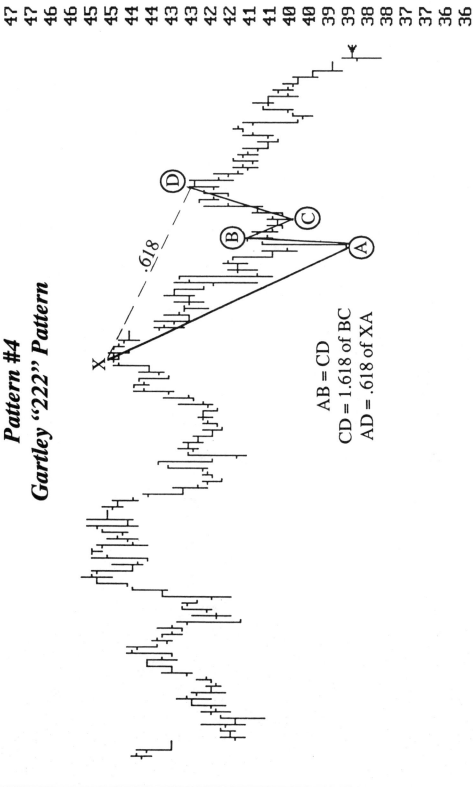

AB = CD
CD = 1.618 of BC
AD = .618 of XA

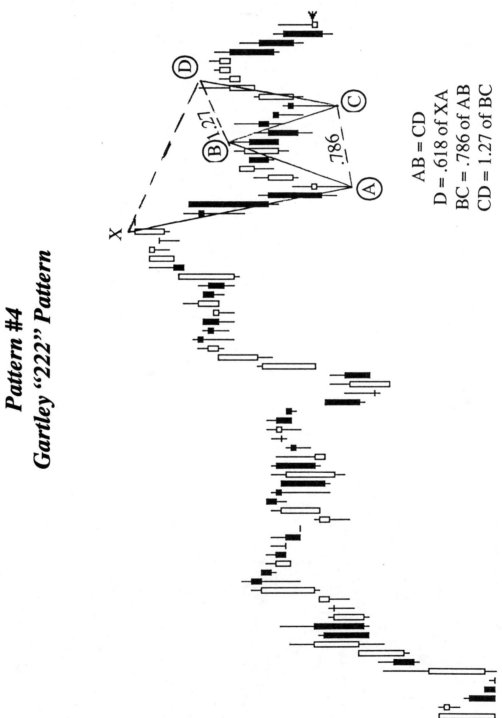

American Express (AXP) Daily

Pattern #4
Gartley "222" Pattern

AB = CD
D = .618 of XA
BC = .786 of AB
CD = 1.27 of BC

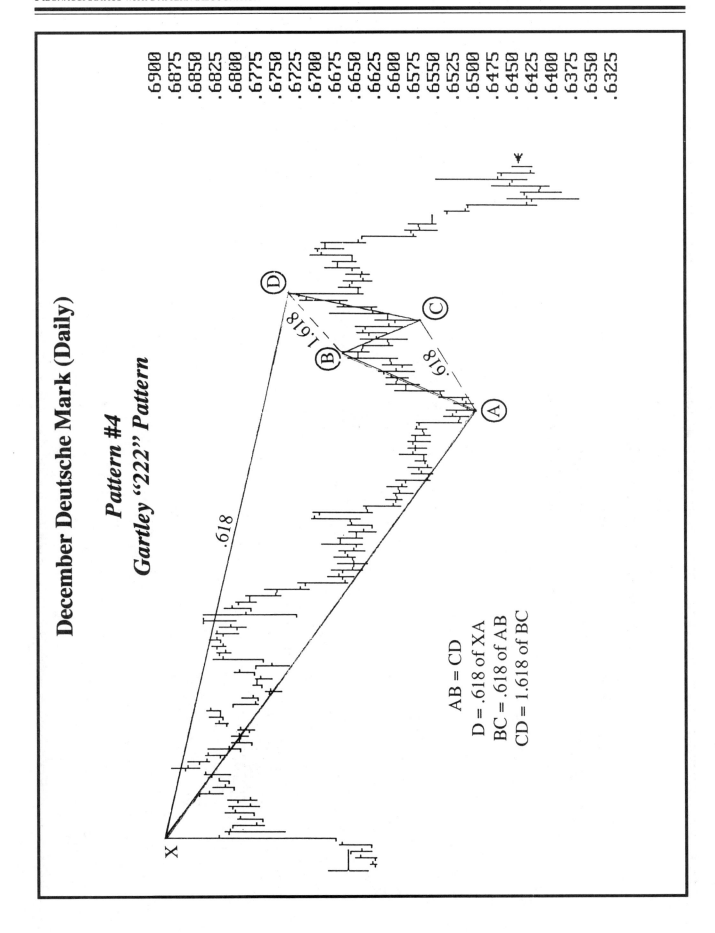

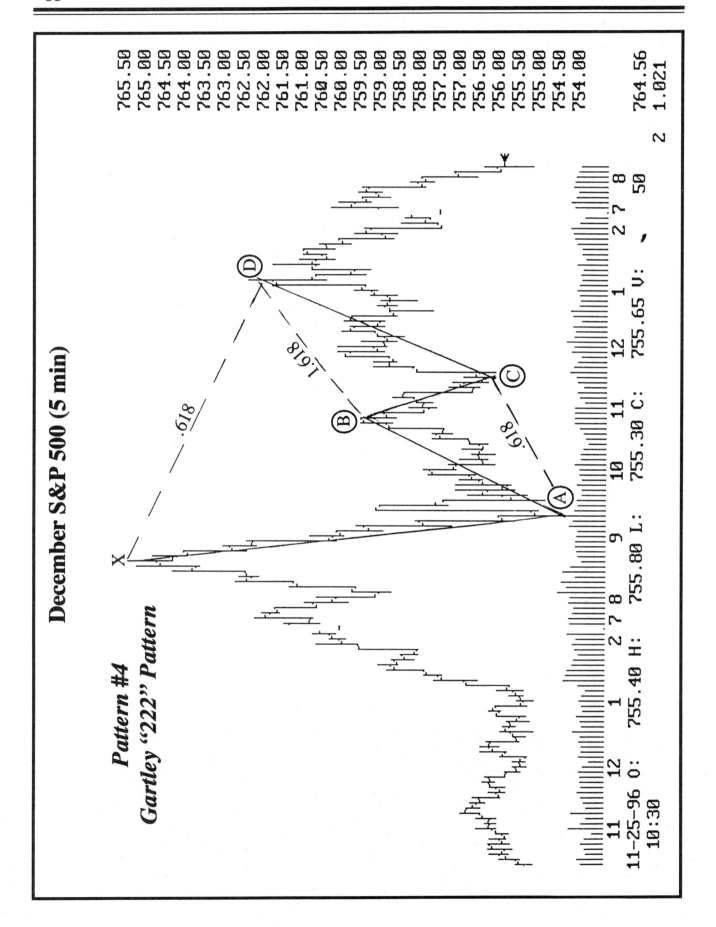

PATTERN #5

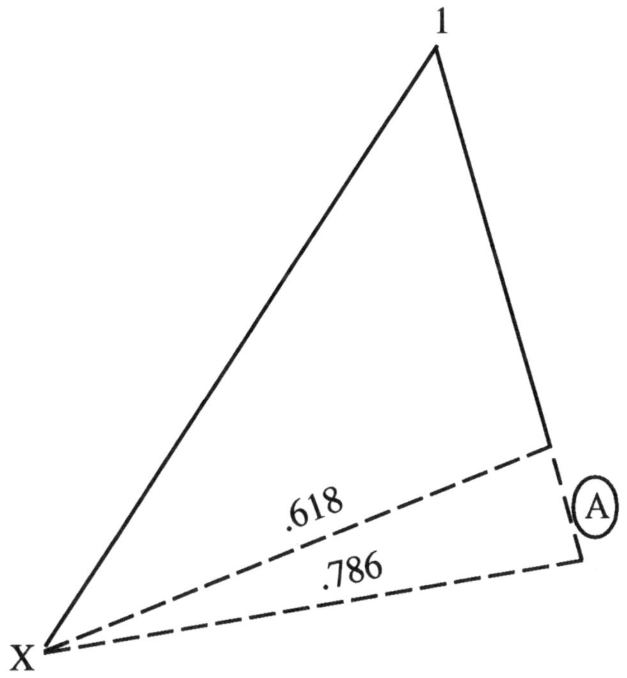

[Diagram: Triangle with vertex 1 at top, X at bottom left, and A at bottom right. Dashed lines from X to A labeled .618 and .786]

1. The time frame between point X and point A will be between 5 and 13 time bars (i.e., 5 min., 30 min., or daily). On rare instances 21 time bars. These are Fibonacci numbers.

2. There are no swing patterns present between points 1 and A.

3. When the move from X to 1 is very explosive, the pullback to point A may only retrace to 38.2% or 50% 1X.

4. If the price difference between the .618 and .786 retracement is greater than the trader is willing to risk, the trader should wait for further confirmation (i.e., a change in momentum or candlestick pattern: *doji, hammer*). In the S&P 500, for example, if the difference between the .618 and .786 numbers is greater than 1.70 points, I will wait for further confirmation to enter the trade.

5. Time periods, the next swing will usually be dramatic to the downside. If the time frame down from point 1 to A is longer than 8 periods, the ensuing pullback will most likely be less dramatic.

6. The trader will never know which of the retracement numbers the market is going to reach. It is the trader's decision to determine how much risk is in the trade.

7. This pattern forces you to trade with the short term trend. You are not trying to pick a top or bottom.

8. After entry, once prices move 61.8% in the direction of the trend, the protective stop should be moved to point A. This gives a risk free trade.

9. The minimum price objective should be the same distance from point A to 1.

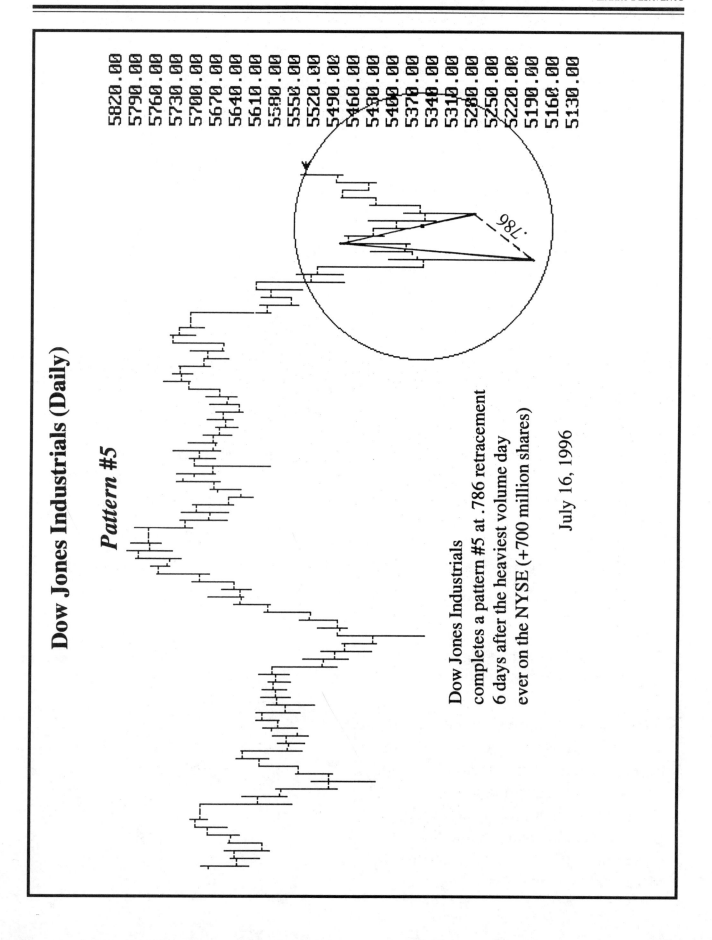

Anhauser Busch (BUD) Daily

Pattern #5

Notice the symmetry of these two #5 patterns in the Dow Jones component. Once you see a pattern you can expect to see it again.

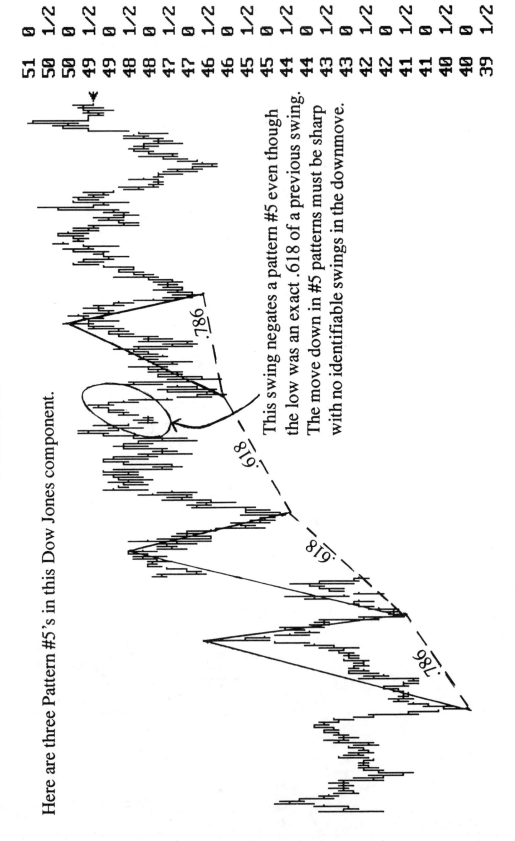

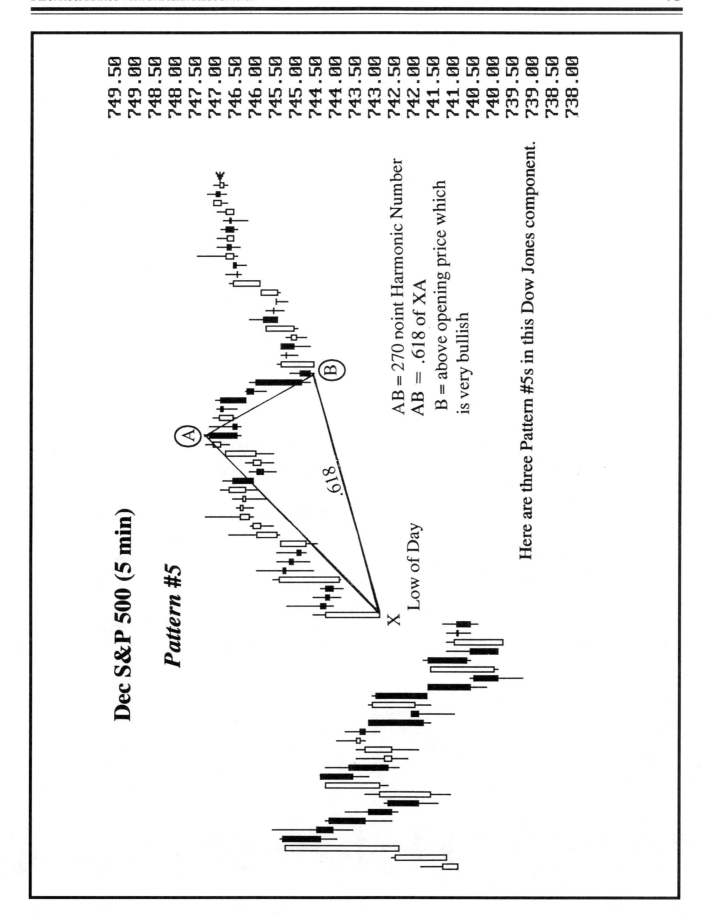

PATTERN #6

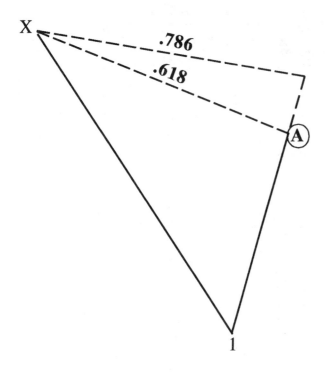

1. The time frame between point X and A will be between 5 and 13 time bars (i.e., 5 min., 30, or daily). On rare instances 21 time bars.

2. There are usually no swing patterns present between points 1 and A.

3. When the move from X to 1 is very explosive, the pullback to point A may only retrace to 38.2% or 50% of 1X.

4. If the price difference between the .618 and .786 retracement is greater than the trader is willing to risk, the trader should wait for further confirmation (i.e, change in momentum or candlestick pattern; doji or hammer). In the S&P 500, for example, if the difference between the .618 and .786 is greater than 170 points I will wait for further confirmation to enter the trade.

5. The time bars between points X and A give a strong clue to the next swing. When the distance from point A is very short, 3 to 5 time periods, the next swing will be explosive to the upside. If the time frame down from point 1 to A is longer than 8 periods, the ensuing rally will most likely not be as strong.

6. The trader will never know which of the retracement numbers the market is going to reach. It is the trader's decision to determine how much risk is in the trade.

7. This pattern forces you to trade with the short term trend. You are not trying to pick a top or bottom.

8. After entry, once prices move 61.8% in the direction of the trend, the protective stop should be moved to point A. This gives a risk free trade.

9. The minimum price objective should be the same distance as point X to 1.

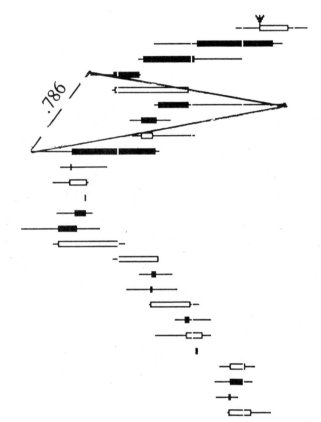

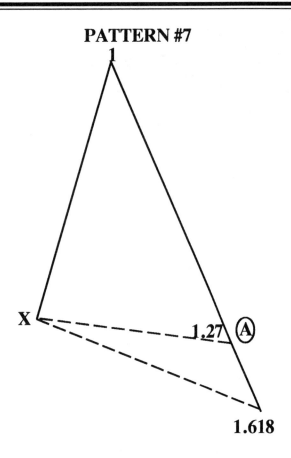

PATTERN #7

1. The time frame between X and point A will be between 5 and 13 time bars (i.e., 5 min., 30 min., daily). On rare occasions 21 time bars.

2. This is a reversal or extension pattern. Expect prices to reverse at point A.

3. If the dollar amount between the 1.27 price and 1.618 price is too great, the trader should wait for more confirmation (i.e., *doji* or *hammer* or another indicator) of an exhaustion move.

4. The thrust down from 1 to A will give a good clue what to expect. If prices get to the 1.27 within 5 bars or less prices will most probably extend to the 1.618.

5. There should be no price swings between point 1 and point A. If there is a price swing Pattern #6 becomes a Gartley 222 pattern.

6. This is a very important pattern when day trading because point X is often the opening price of the day.

7. When prices react in the direction of the trade, the protective stop should be raised to break even.

8. Profit objective should be the total distance between points 1 and A.

Fibonacci Ratios with Pattern Recognition

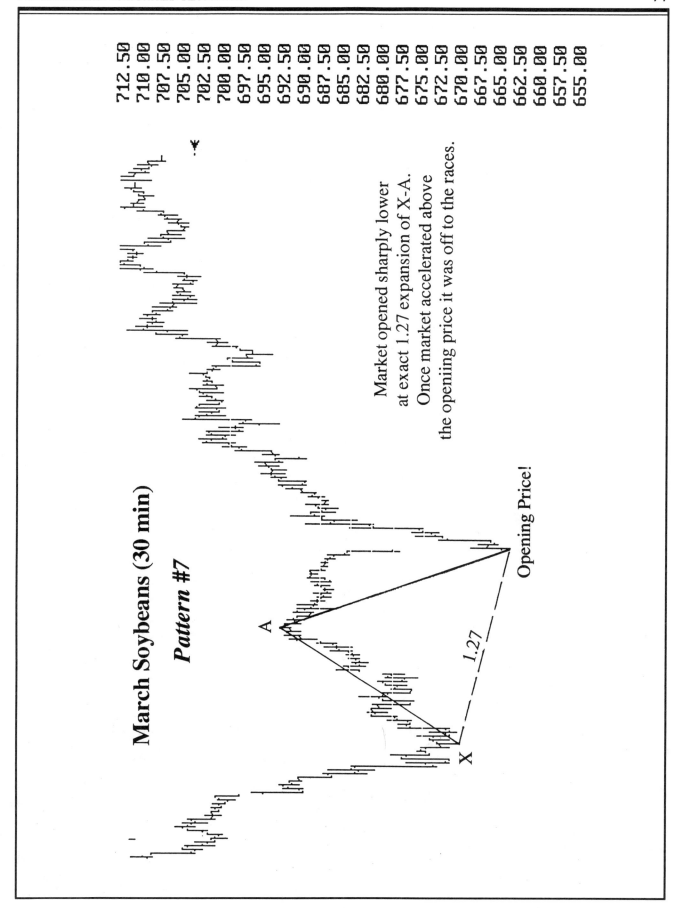

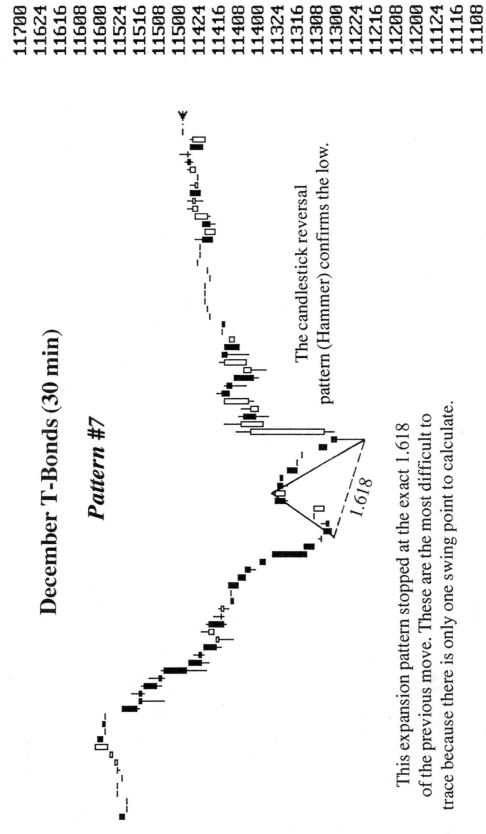

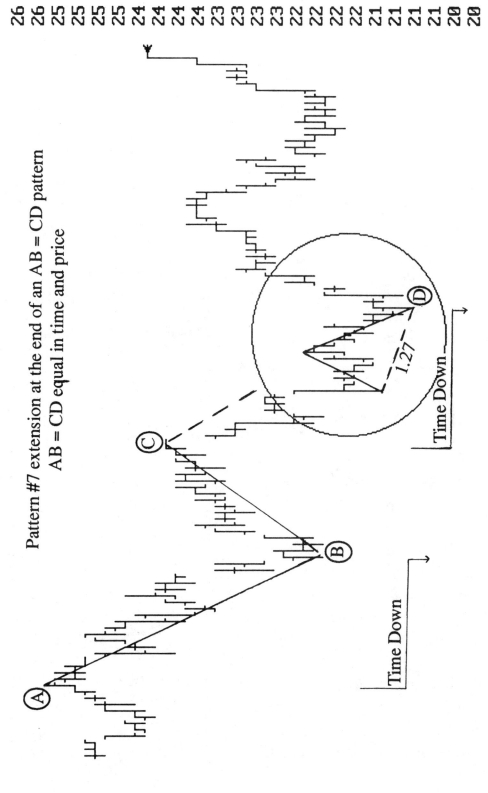

PATTERN #8

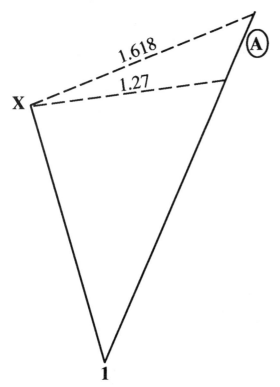

1. The time frame between X and point A will be 5 and 13 time bars (i.e., 5 min., 30 min., daily). On rare occasions 21 time bars.

2. This is a reversal or extension pattern. Expect prices to reverse at point A.

3. If the dollar amount between the 1.27 price and 1.618 price is too great, the trader should wait for more confirmation (i.e., *doji* or *hammer* or another indicator) of an exhaustion move.

4. The thrust up from 1 to A will give a good clue what to expect. If prices get to the 1.27 within 5 bars or less prices will most probably extend to the 1.618.

5. There should be no price swings between point 1 and point A. If there is a price swing, Pattern #6 becomes a Gartley "222" pattern.

6. This is a very important pattern when day trading because point X is often the opening price of the day.

7. When prices react in the direction of the trade, the protective stop should be raised to break even.

8. Profit objective should be the total distance between points 1 and A.

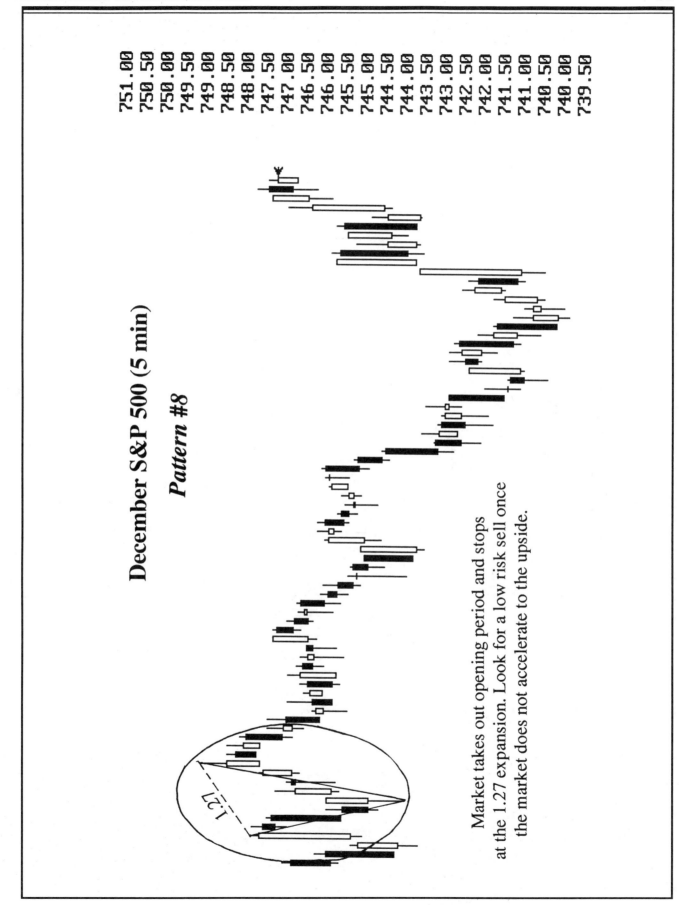

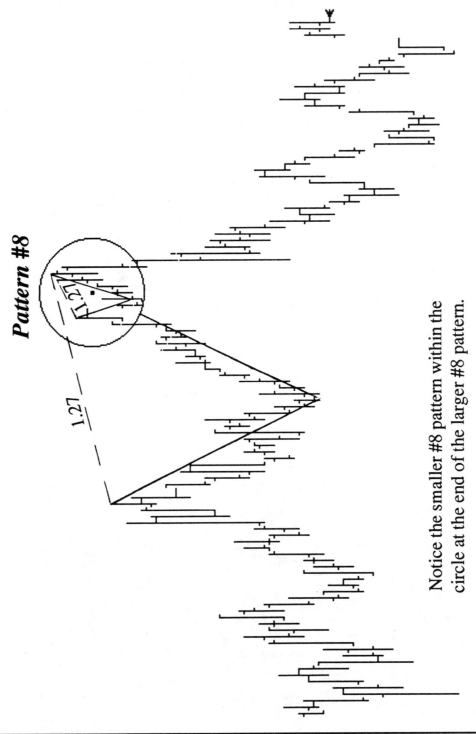

Notice the smaller #8 pattern within the circle at the end of the larger #8 pattern.

Fibonacci Ratios with Pattern Recognition

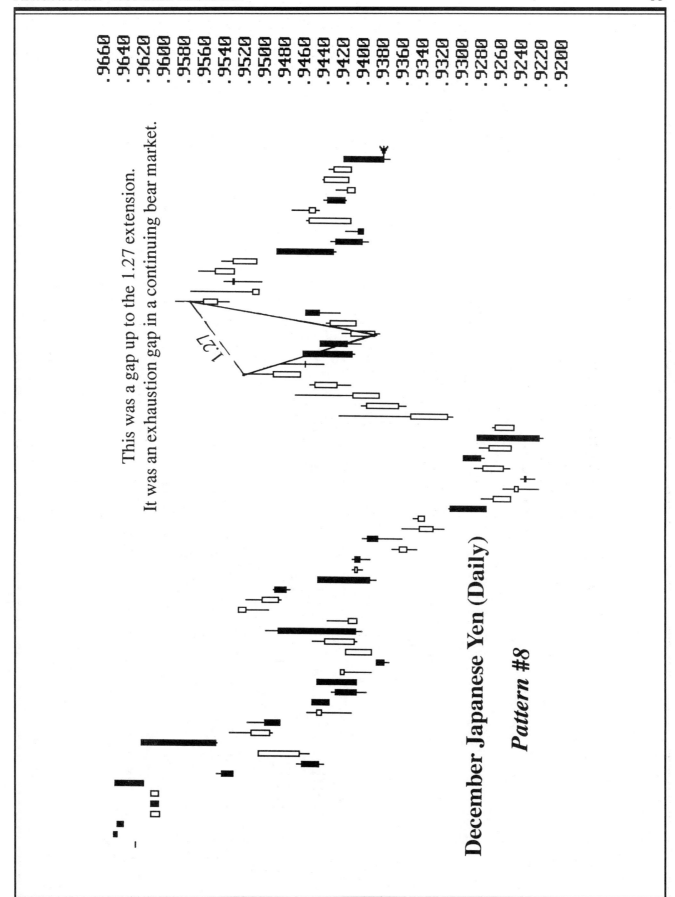

December Japanese Yen (Daily)

Pattern #8

This was a gap up to the 1.27 extension. It was an exhaustion gap in a continuing bear market.

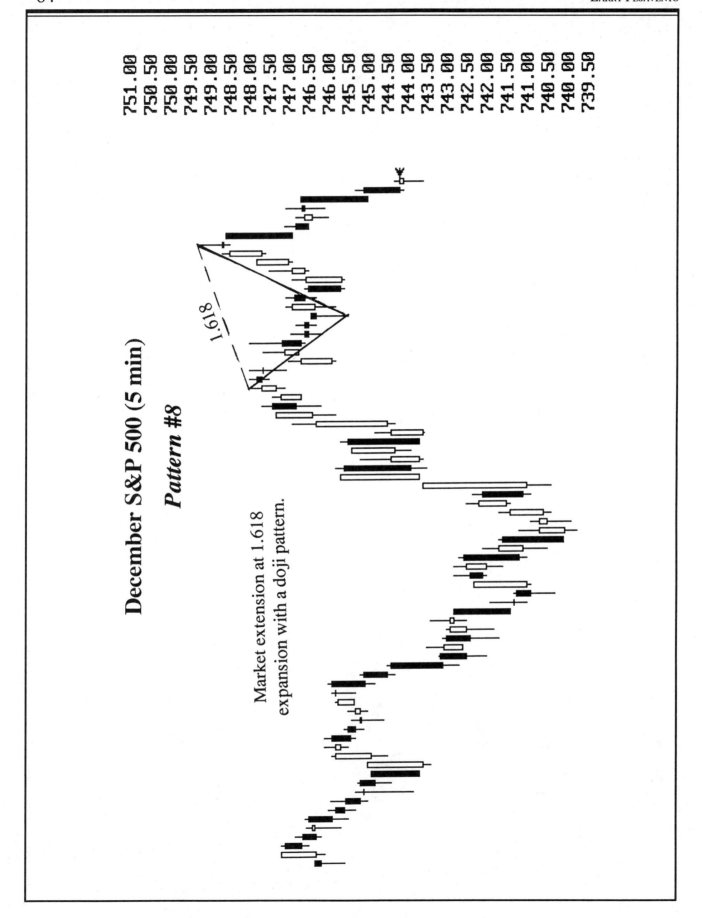

PATTERN #9
THREE DRIVES TO A TOP

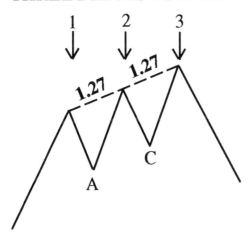

1. The pattern should be easily identified. If you have to force the numbers, it is probably not this pattern.

2. Symmetry is the key to this pattern. Points 2 and 3 should be 1.27 or 1.618 price expansions of the A and C swings.

3. The time frames from point A to 2 and C to 3 should be symmetrical.

4. If there is a big price gap in this pattern at any time it is a sign that the 3 drive pattern is wrong and the trader should wait for further confirmation that a top is in progress.

5. Price swings A and C will usually be at the .618 or .786 retracement of the previous swing. When the market is a vertical (blow off) pattern, these retracements will only be .382.

6. Three drives to a top is a rare pattern.

After you start to see this patttern, it will be much easier to interpret. Don't search for the pattern, it should **jump** out at you as you study the chart.

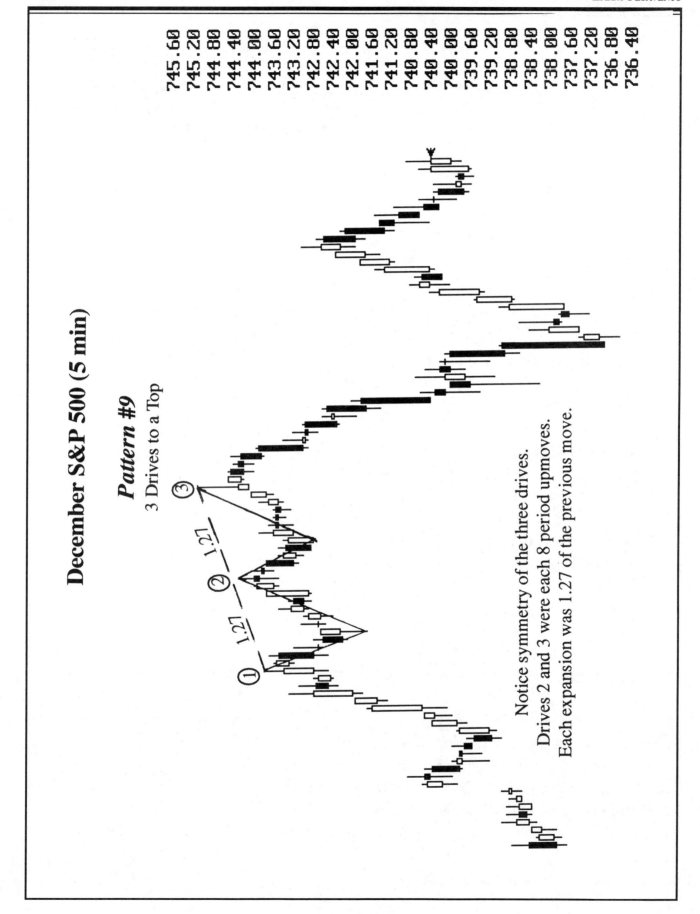

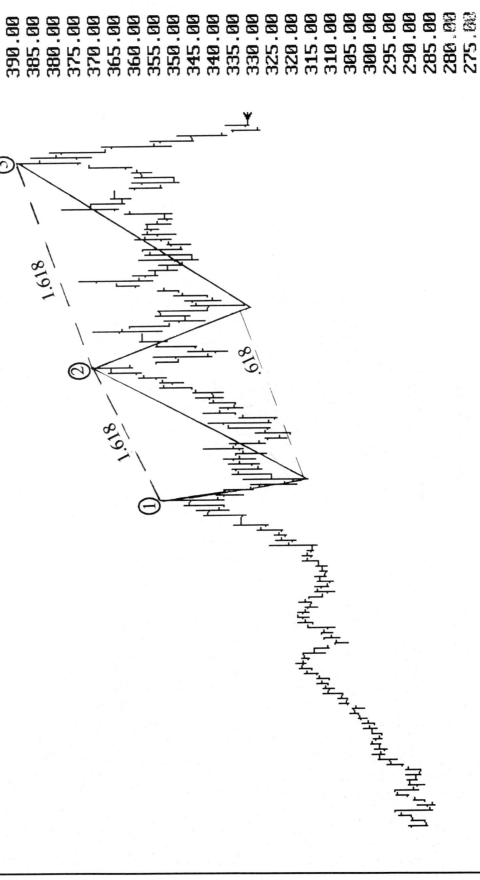

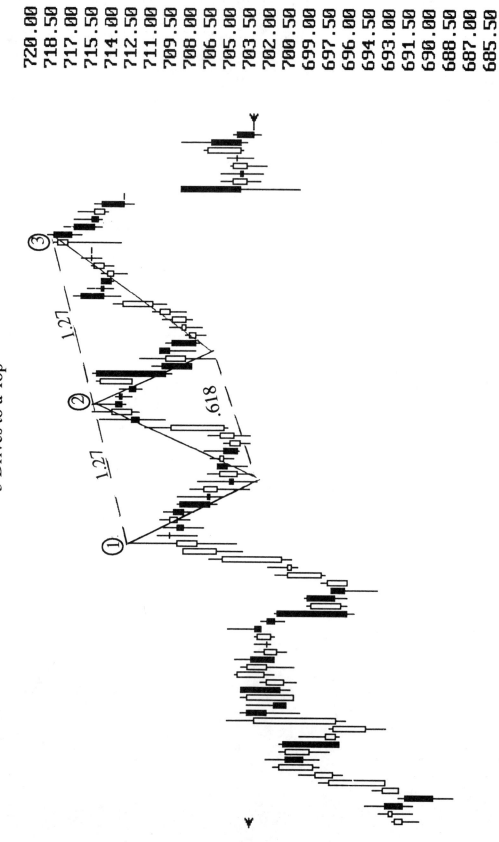

PATTERN #10
THREE DRIVES TO A BOTTOM

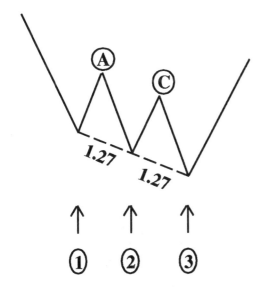

1. The pattern should easily be identified. If you have to force the numbers, it is probably not this pattern.

2. Symmetry is the key to this pattern. Points 2 and 3 should be 1.27 or 1.618 price expansions of the A and C swings.

3. The time frames from point A to 2 and C to 3 should be symmetrical.

4. If there is a big price gap in this pattern at any time it is a sign that the 3 drive pattern is wrong and the trader should wait for further confirmation that a bottom is in progress.

5. Price swings A and C will usually be at the .618 or .786 retracement of the previous swing. When the market is in a free fall (exhaustion) these retracements will only be .382.

6. Three drives to a bottom is a rare pattern. After you start to see this pattern, it will be much easier to interpret. Don't search for the pattern, it should **jump** out at you as you study the chart.

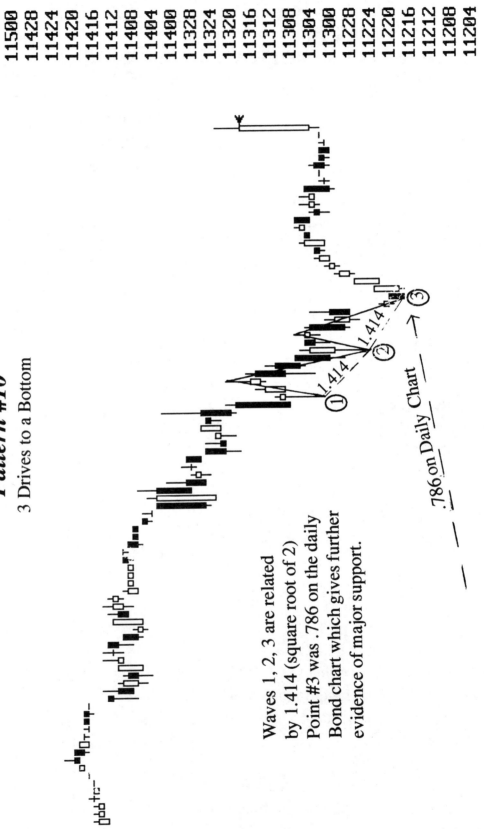

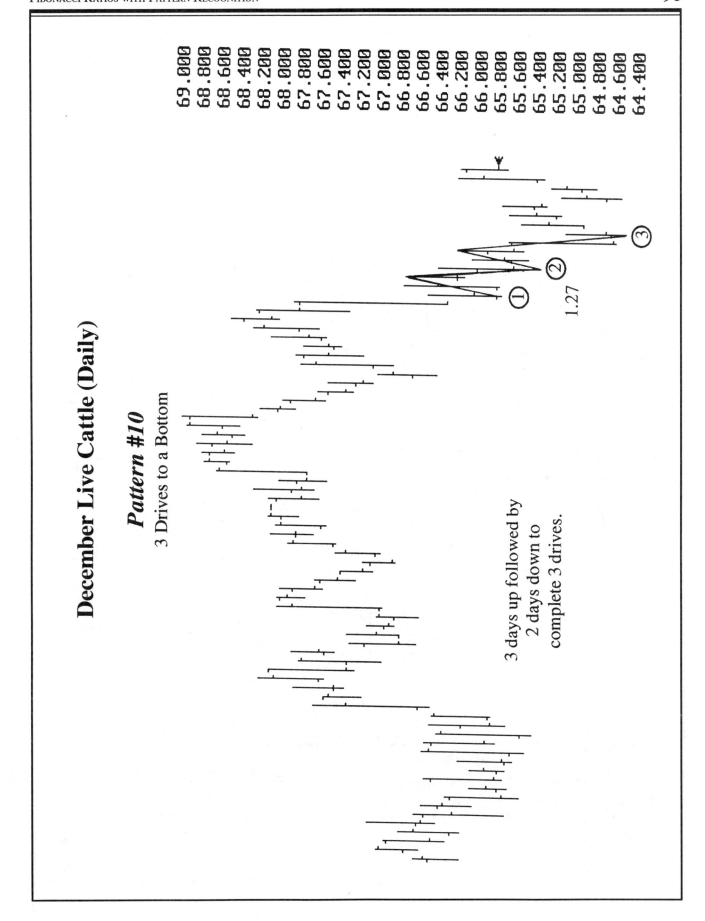

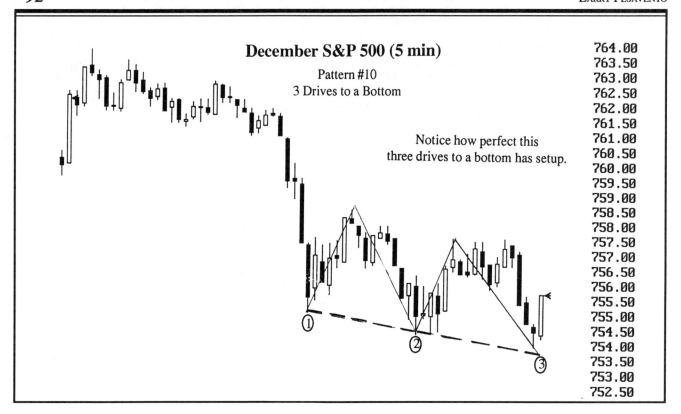

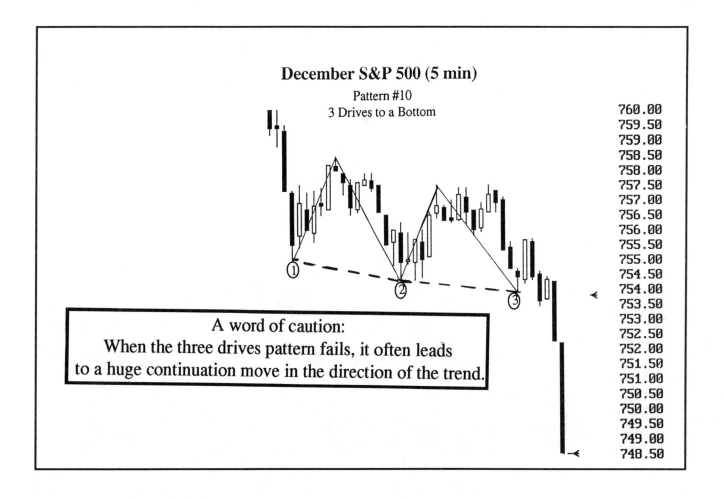

CLASSICAL CHART PATTERNS USING RATIO AND PROPORTION

Those of you who follow the standard trading pattern discussed in technical analysis may find this section interesting. I have selected the four more common patterns traders encounter. If the trader will analyze the pattern using the ratios discussed in this book, it will most probably be enlightening besides increasing probabilitites of a profitable trade.

1. Head and Shoulders Pattern (Bottoms and Tops)

2. Double Bottoms and Tops

3. Symmetrical Triangles (Broadening Tops and Bottoms)

4. Dynamite Triangles

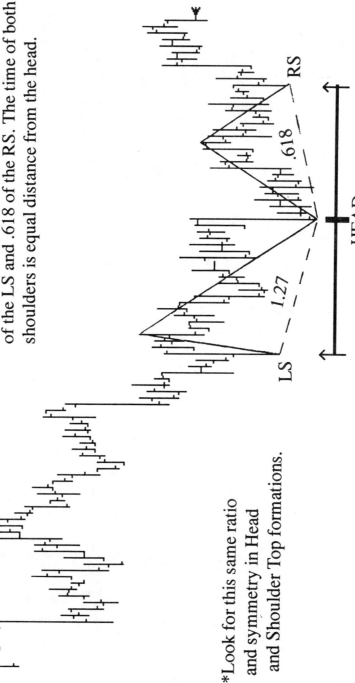

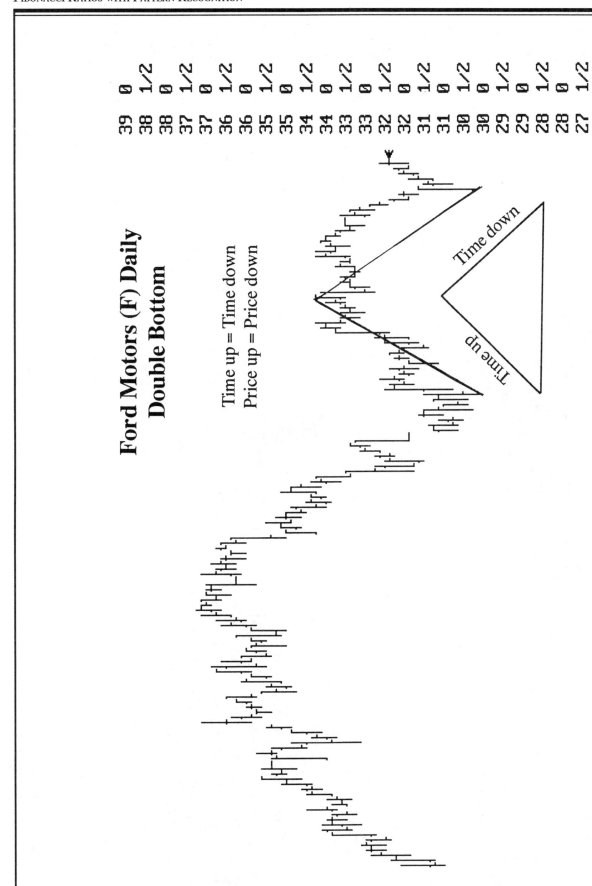

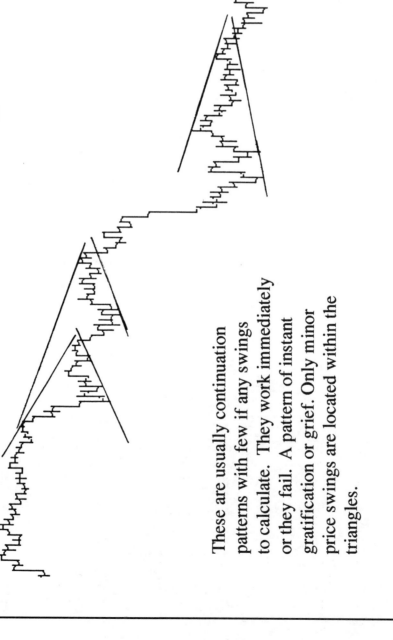

December S&P 500 (5 min) Dynamite Triangles (*descending*)

These are usually continuation patterns with few if any swings to calculate. They work immediately or they fail. A pattern of instant gratification or grief. Only minor price swings are located within the triangles.

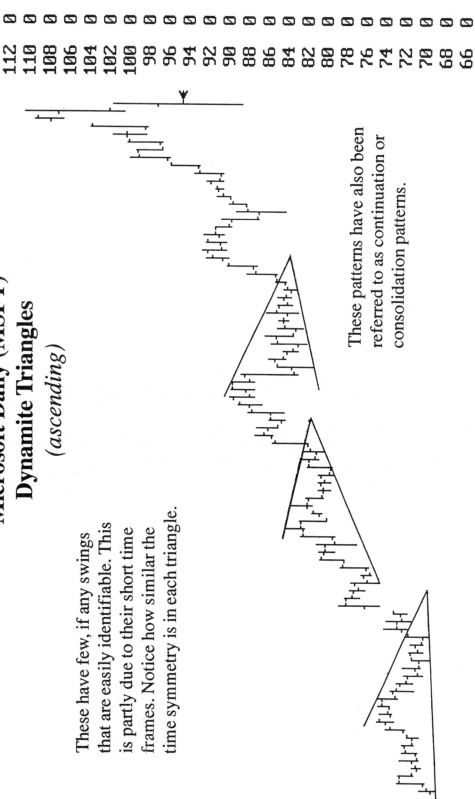

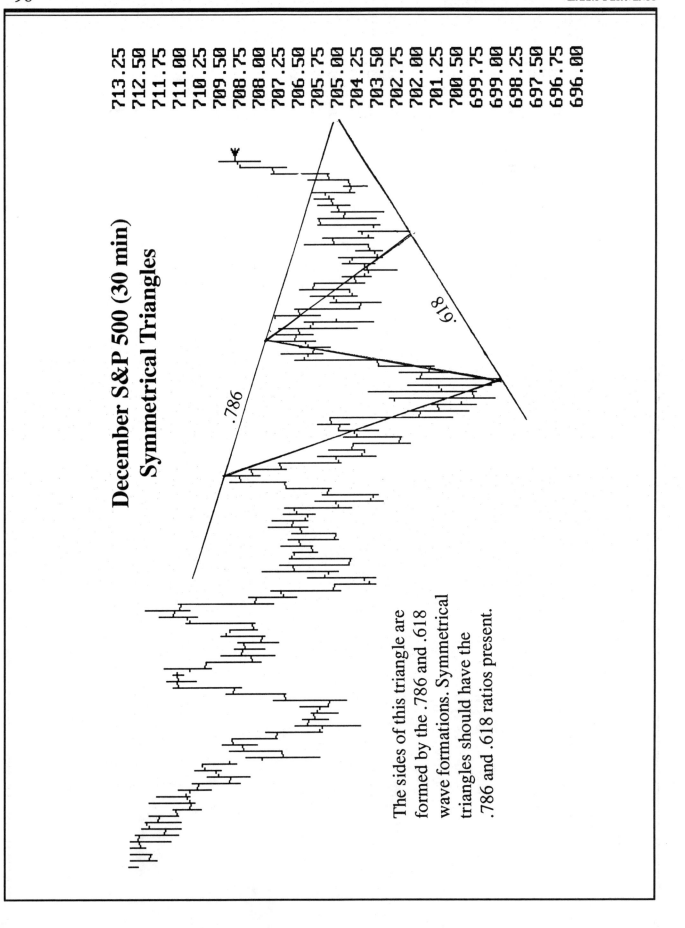

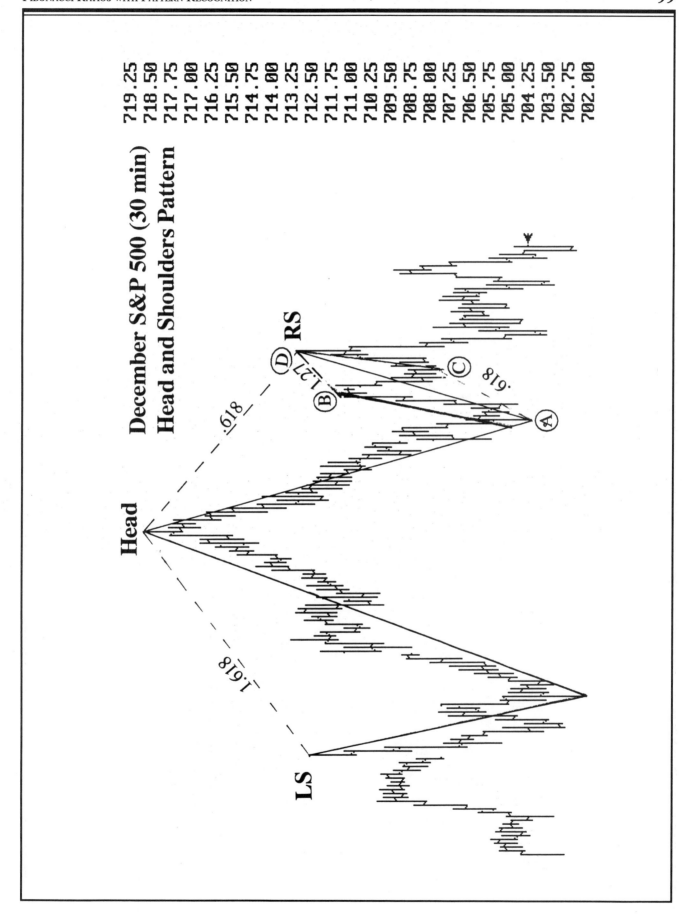

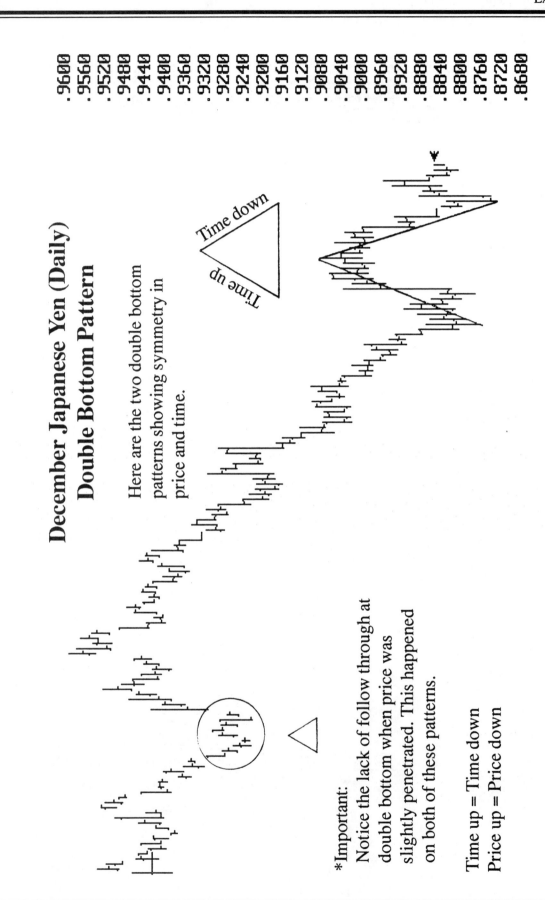

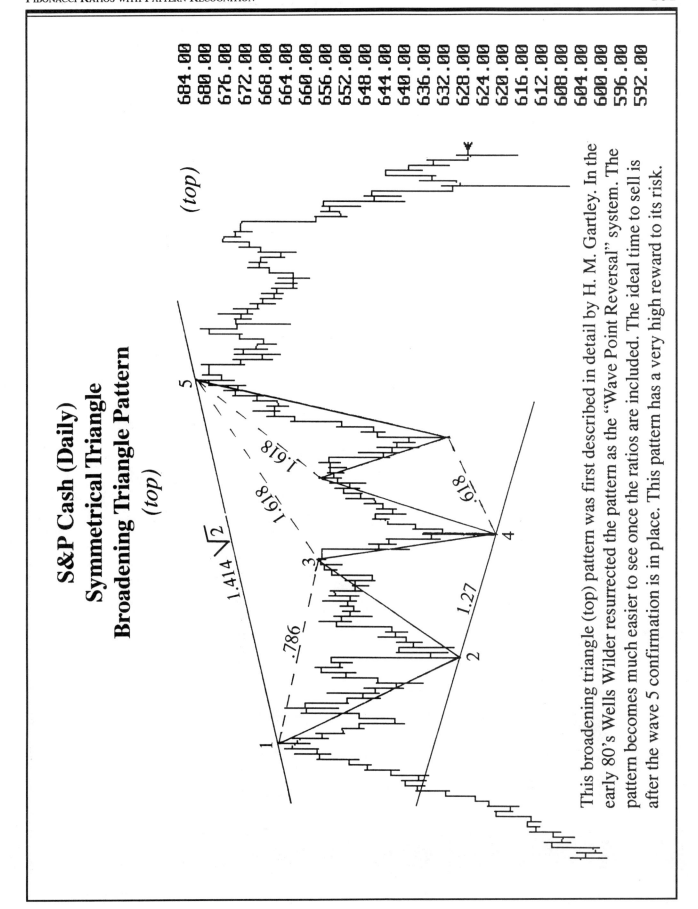

**S&P Cash (Daily)
Symmetrical Triangle
Broadening Triangle Pattern**
(top)

This broadening triangle (top) pattern was first described in detail by H. M. Gartley. In the early 80's Wells Wilder resurrected the pattern as the "Wave Point Reversal" system. The pattern becomes much easier to see once the ratios are included. The ideal time to sell is after the wave 5 confirmation is in place. This pattern has a very high reward to its risk.

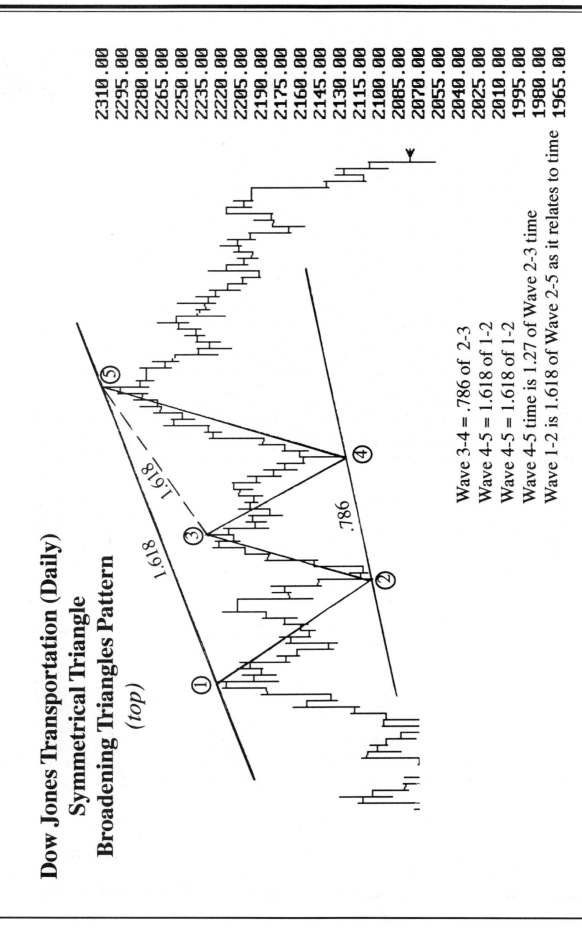

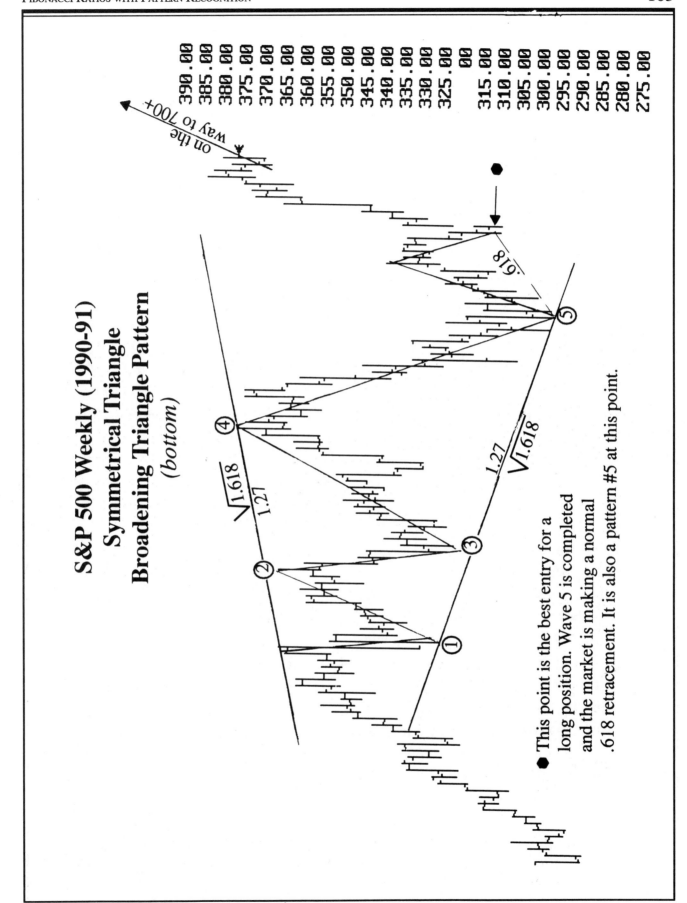

BONUS PATTERN: THE BUTTERFLY

TOP

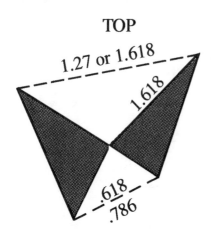

BOTTOM

Bryce Gilmore and I discovered this pattern while we were running analysis routines on his *Wave Trader Software*. It is a very powerful pattern and is seen at significant tops and bottoms only. The "Butterfly" beauty lies in its symmetry. It is my second favorite pattern. (First is Gartley "222").

When several of my close friends reviewed this book for me they suggested that I omit the Butterfly pattern. I already knew my response to the suggestion. I firmly believe that you can give the trading public the *Holy Grail* and they still won't grasp the principle. The reasons for this are probably related to a general level of skepticism and inability to actually do the work involved. This pattern is far removed from any *Holy Grail*! Find a few on your own and make your own judgement. I know you will find the time well spent.

CHARACTERISTICS OF THE "BUTTERFLY" PATTERN

1. It is formed by the connecting of two triangles.

2. An AB = CD pattern is present in the extension move.

3. The extension move can be either 1.27 or 1.618. Any move beyond 1.618 negates this pattern. Should this occur, a very strong continuation move is in progress.

4. It is found only at significant tops and bottoms.

5. The time bar relationship usually is in ratio and proportion to the price bar.

6. It is correct more than 80% of the time.

7. The retracement moves inside the butterfly will usually contain .618 and .786 moves.

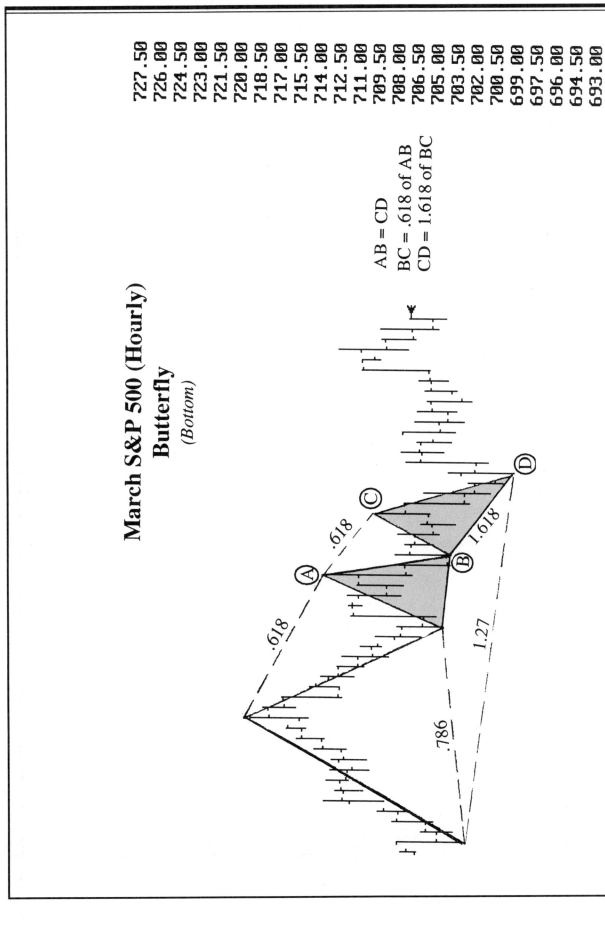

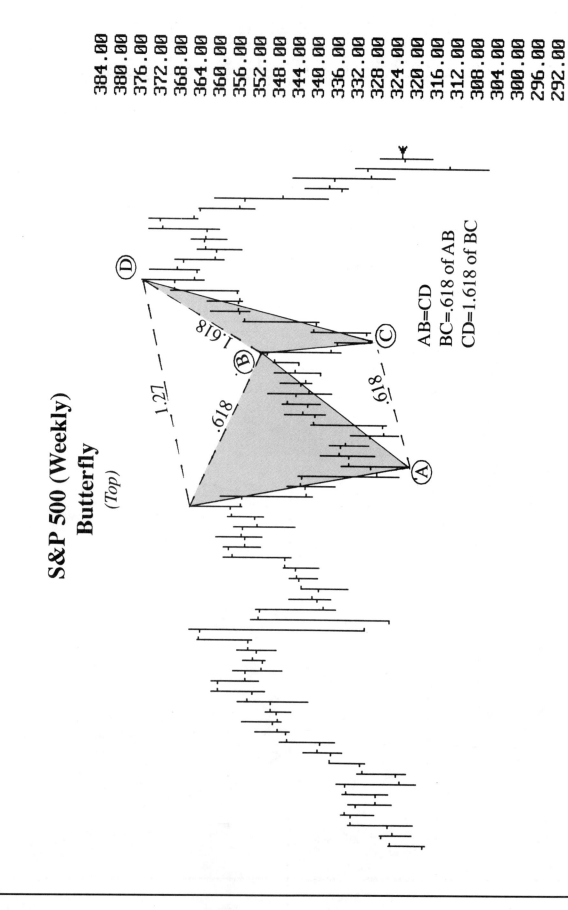

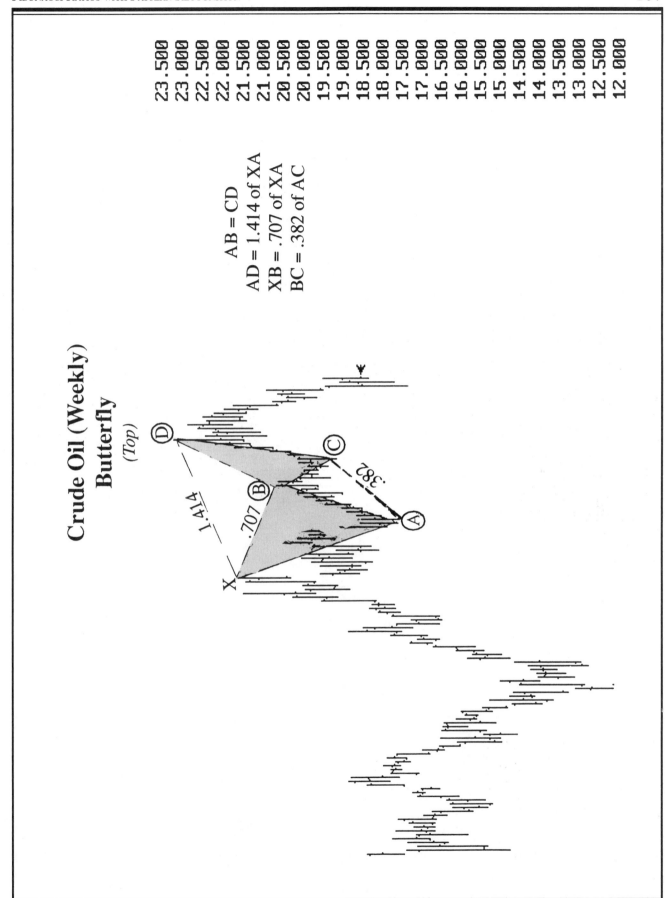

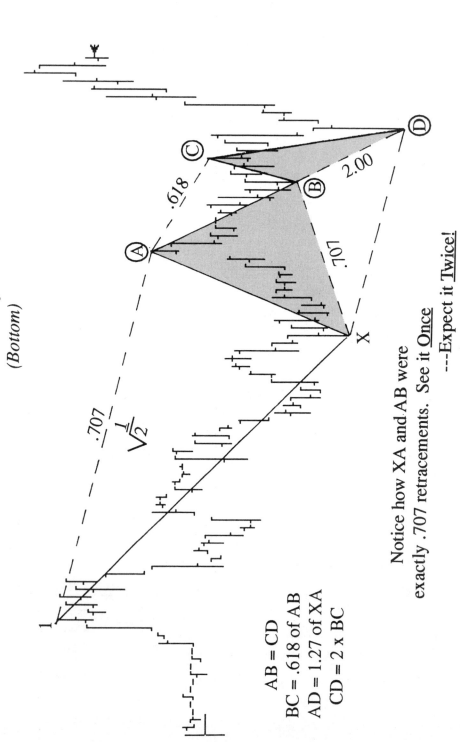

THE OPENING PRICE

I first met John Hill of the **Commodity Research Institute** in Hendersonville, North Carolina in late 1974 or early 1975. At that time, I was recovering from a tremendous loss in cattle, soybean oil and soybean meal. I was long many contracts during the 1974 October break. I started with nothing, but ran it up to a great deal of money. I then realized that I had the ability to make that kind of money. However, I neglected to realize that I confused success with a bull market and I was unprepared when the bear market finally came.

During these last 14 years, John and I remained good friends and shared numerous good trading ideas. In 1982 I went to John's ranch in Hendersonville and spent two weeks with him looking at various ways to trade the markets. One of the best discoveries we made was a computer study which revealed to us the principle called *Trading in the Direction of the Opening Price*. We worked two solid weeks in several different markets, relating the opening price to the price action of that day. It is one of the most amazing discoveries I used as a technical indicator in trading commodities.

Several years later, Earl Haddady of the Haddady-Sibbett Corporation published the same statistics in a book called *The Importance of the Opening Price*. We heartily recommend this book to anyone interested in trading commodities and especially to those involved in day trading. It puts a tremendous advantage on your side when you're trading in the direction of the opening price.

The principle behind the importance of the opening price probably stems from the fact that the markets are open only six hours a day. That leaves 18 hours for decision making to occur. When you consider the fact that the foreign markets are open in Hong Kong, Tokyo, Singapore, Sidney, London and Amsterdam, you get an even greater flavor of what occurs during the 18 hours when our markets are closed. It is my opinion that decisions are made during the 18 hours that affect the opening of our market. I realize that most of the volume is not done on the opening— it is done during the complete day. However, to explain how the opening price is so significant, one must remember that these people have been making thought decisions and analytical decisions during the past 18 hours in order to come up with strategies for the following days.

The Opening Price Principle is this: the opening price will be at or near the high or low of that day 85-90 percent of the time. In other words, the price at the opening will be either within 10 percent either the high or the low of the day on that particular day. There are two ways that you can prove this principle to yourself. First, take a commodity chart like *Commodity Perspective* or *Futures Charts*, something that shows the opening price which would be the small left-hand bar on the daily bar chart—not the closing price, but the left-hand side which is the opening price. Take a red pencil and draw a little circle around the opening price. Continue that through the life of the contract. Set the chart down and you'll see that the high or the low of the day was the opening price approximately eight or nine times out of 10. The second way to test the importance of the opening price is to use the day trading charts—that is Intraday charts—if you have access to them. Using an intraday chart, mark the opening price and draw a line across the time zone for the rest of the day--a horizontal line where the opening price is indicated. You'll be surprised how often prices meander around that opening price whether it is the high or the low of the day. Even when it's not the high or the low of the day, the opening price seems to be some kind of harmonic or equilibrium price that the market bounces against several times during the day.

Armed with this information, a day trader and, actually, a position trader can enter the market to his advantage with probabilities on his side. The charts on the following pages show examples of how to use the opening price advantage as part of your armamentarium for strategy in entering a market for a position trade and also for profiting on a day trading basis. Keep in mind that this technique does not work all of the time, but that it does put probability in your favor a great deal of the time.

There is an important concept here to remember: forget about the closing price of yesterday. It means absolutely nothing when you're dealing with the opening price concept. Whether the price gaps up or the price gaps down is of no consequence to you when you are using the opening price to enter a market. You must forget the closing price of the previous day; the opening price is your focus, especially when day trading. Whenever I taught this principle, students always seemed to want to hang onto the closing price of yesterday. **You must remember not to use yesterday's closing price when using the opening price principle.**

You will see that this technique does get easier with practice as you become more accustomed to its use. The charts on the next several pages present examples of how to use the opening price in conjunction with patterns and pattern recognition formations in order to set up day trading probabilities. You may want to use the "Key of the Day" (Opening + High + Low divided by 3) with this technique. If prices are above *Key of Day*, only go long. If below *Key of Day*, only go short.

Keep in mind that in day trading—and also position trading—you must be concerned with both the Price and the Time Axis. Some people who day trade will inadvertently lose money because they forget about the Time Axis. They think they are trading just for several days when, in fact, they put a trade on for a day trade and it turns into a position trade which gaps the opposite of what position they are holding, resulting in a loss. When you are day trading, you should be out on the close. If you are position trading, you should position yourself for a longer term move somewhere in the neighborhood of three days to three months, depending on your style of trading.

The first example of how to use the opening price is illustrated on page 112; this chart shows the market opened at Price A then began to react downward and continue down. People who bought near the high of the day are now concerned whether the market is going back up through the high or have a key reversal to the downside. As you can see, after a period of time, the market reached support. This support is at a major Fibonacci number, the (.618) retracement off the opening price. The market has held there and has now started to move higher.

One of our favorite day trading techniques is to buy that (.618) retracement from the opening price with a stop at the (.85) retracement. In other words, if the market dropped more than 25 percent below the (.618) you would be able to say that you were wrong; your stop limitation is very small and you would be able to profit as the market moved higher. As evidenced in this example, the market did, in fact, move higher and you turned a profit at the end of the day.

It is also important to get a very fair commission rate when day trading. As $25 - $30 range is completely acceptable for grains, bonds, Standards and Poors and just about any other commodity. Good volatility is essential when day trading. Trade the markets that are quite volatile and highly active with a great deal of volume. This will be covered in greater detail in another section.

The second example of how to use the opening price is illustrated on page 113.
Note the opening price. The market breaks rapidly and then starts to rally back toward the opening price. Again, the market rallies back to the Fibonacci number, (.618), and then resumes its move to the downside. These two examples demonstrate that if a trader is patient and waits for this particular pattern to unfold, the probabilities are in his favor in a twofold manner. First, he is trading in the direction of the opening price. It meanders in the direction the trend is going to be in. It will be in his favor seven or eight times out of ten. Secondly, he's trading in the direction of the trend and selling into a rally at a very strong mathematical point where the risk is quantified because, if the market continues to go up, it will be stopped out with a very small loss. The probabilities of these particular patterns working are better than seven out of 10.

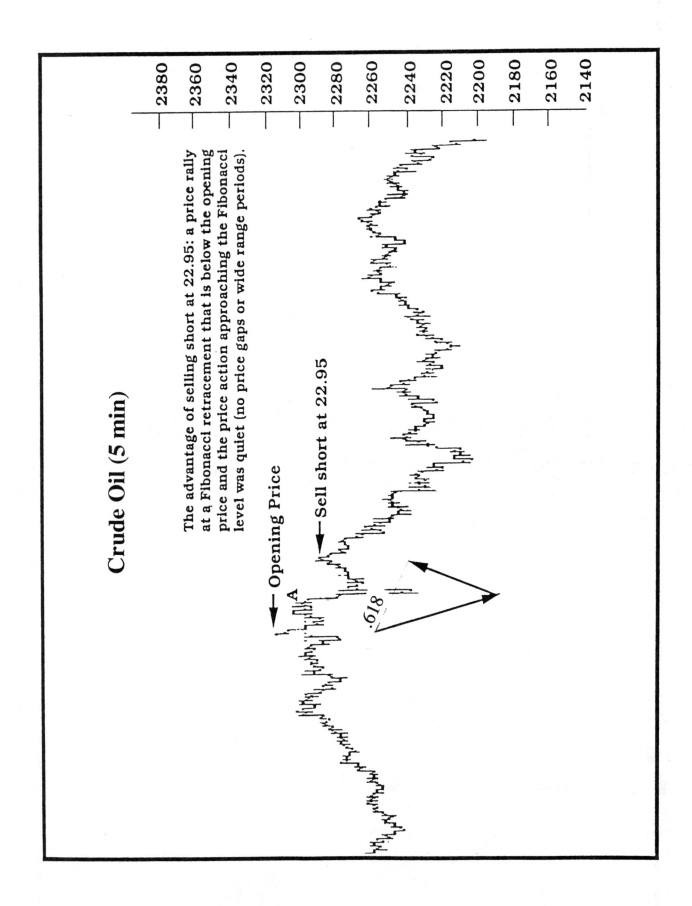

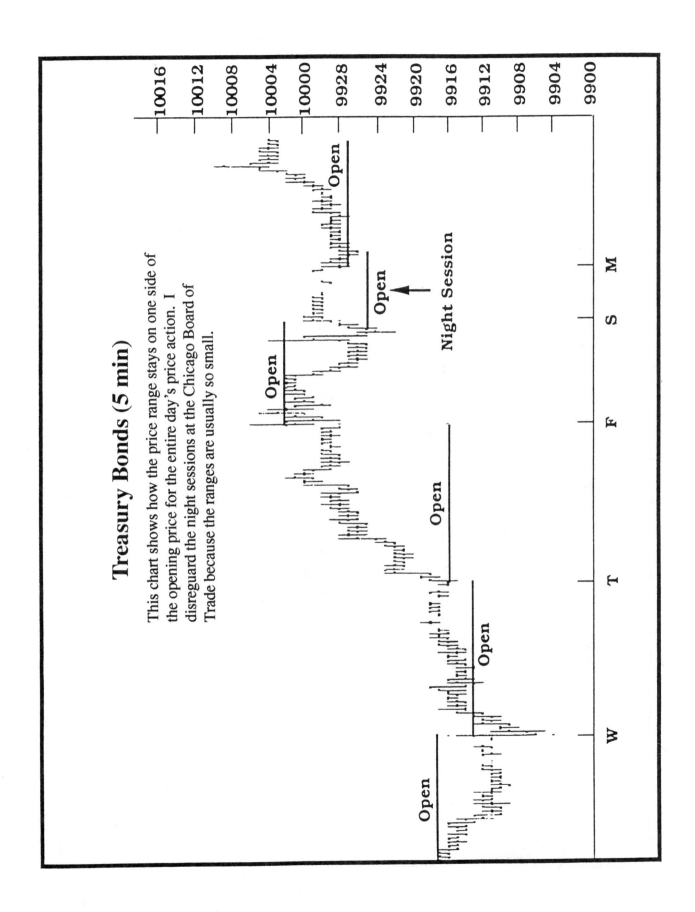

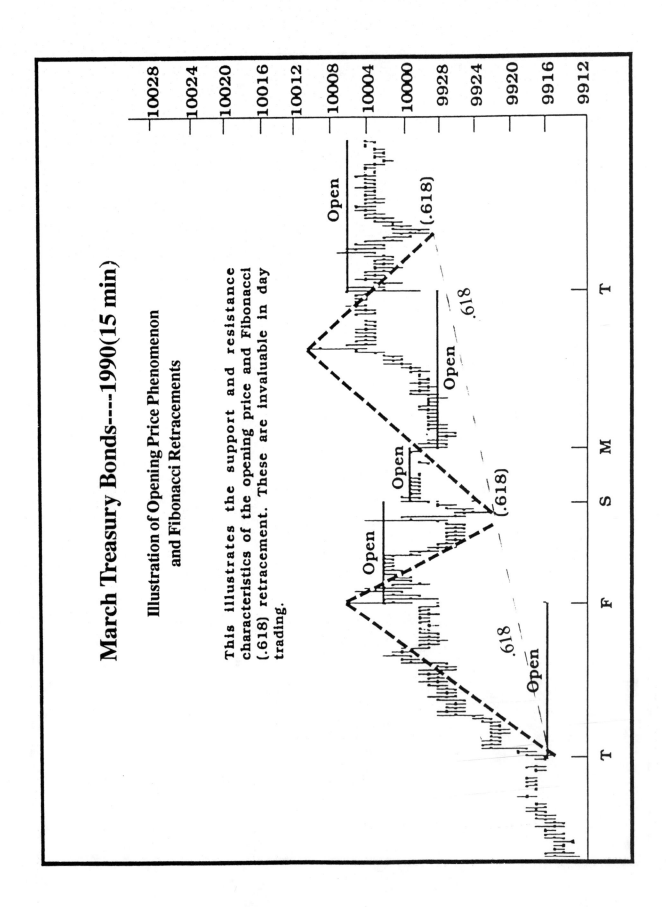

Fibonacci Ratios with Pattern Recognition

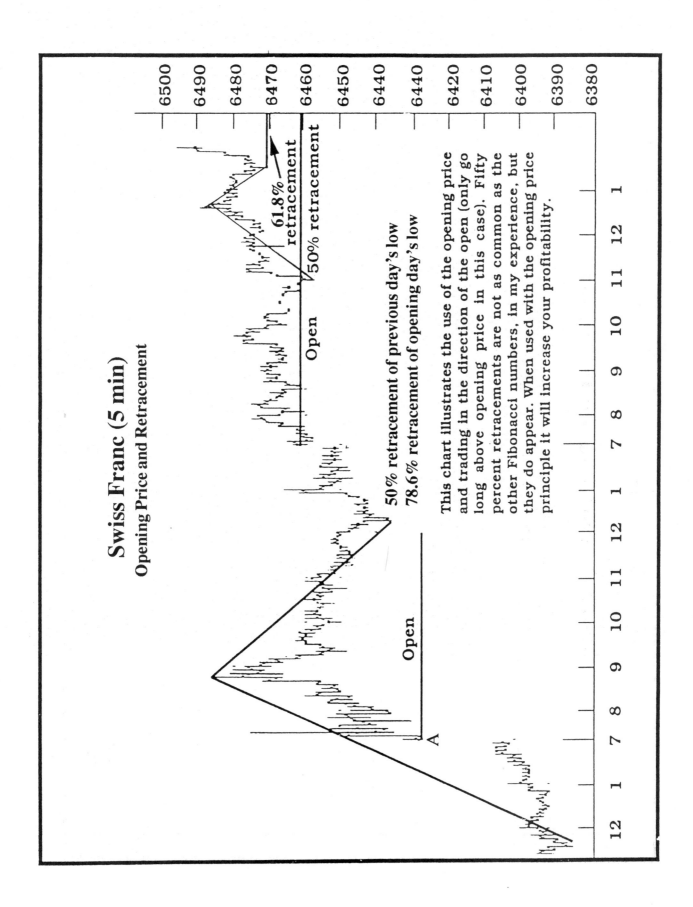

Swiss Franc (5 min)
Opening Price and Retracement

This chart illustrates the use of the opening price and trading in the direction of the open (only go long above opening price in this case). Fifty percent retracements are not as common as the other Fibonacci numbers, in my experience, but they do appear. When used with the opening price principle it will increase your profitability.

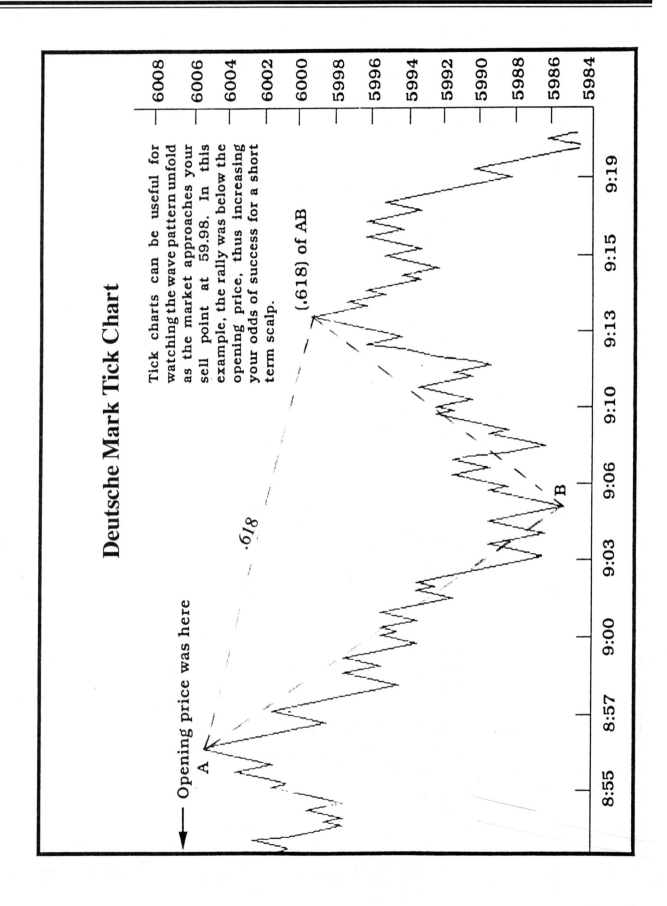

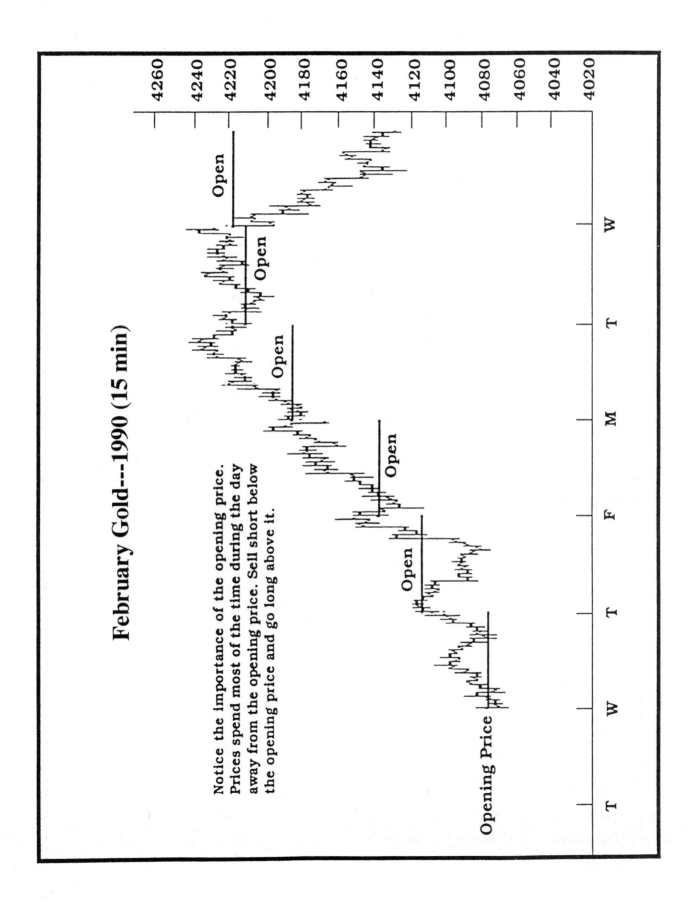

ENTRY TECHNIQUES

Here are some of my favorite entry techniques used in conjunction with the geometric patterns. They are listed in their order of importance (importance to me!)

1. **The Shapiro Iteration** as described in the following pages.

2. **Limit Orders** - Placed a few ticks above or below the exact geometric price measurements. A predetermined stop loss (approxiamtely $600) is placed at the same time.

3. **Candlestick Patterns** - These patterns graphically display the importance of the trading range for that time emphazing the opening price. Here are four usable patterns:

   A. **Tweezers** - This formation is the equivalent of a double bottom. Tweezers occur when 2 lines have equal highs or lows in succession. They help to quantify risk at the completion of the geometric patterns.

   B. **Doji's** - The market opened and closed at the same price after making the highs and lows. They occur when the market is in transition from bullish to bearish mode or vice versa. Doji's are even more important at the end of a geometric pattern. This is also true when they occur after very volatile markets. It is a sign that ALL of the market players --bulls and bears-- are nervous.

   C. **Hammer's** - The hammer is a period when the market has met strong support after a sharp sell off. It gets its name from "hammering out a bottom." A hammer should be twice the length of the candle. Hammer should be esthetically easy to see. If you have a doubt, it is probably not a hammer.

   D. **Shooting Stars**--These are accompanied by an upside gap on the opening with the market closing near the lower end of the trading range. These are particularly useful entry techniques at the end of the geometric pattern. They appear as the opposite of the hanging man.

Many of the candlestick patterns may be helpful as well. I only use these four because they seem to go hand in hand with the geometric patterns.

4. The Volatility Stop Entry Technique

The Volatility Stop calculates the volatility by using the average range of the price bar. It is calculated by multiplying the average range by a contstant. The value is added to the lowest close when short, and subtracted from the highest when long:

Range = (Range x (N-1)) + High - Low /N

Short = Lowest Close + Range x C

Long = Highest Close - Range x C

My experience is to use the Volatility Stop in strongly trending markets. It is an excellent entry technique and in most instances will be superior to valid trend line breaks, or channel breakouts. The reverse stop also acts to quantify risk as it relates to volatility. The constants should be kept between 2.5 and 4.0.

THE SHAPIRO ITERATION

When I day trade and use only one calculation to decide on an entry or exit value, I apply what I like to call the "Shapiro Iteration" before putting on the trade. It involves waiting one bar value of whatever the time value is of the chart I am using to decide on the trade (I wait five minutes if I am using a five minute chart to make trading decisions, 30 minutes if I am using a 30 minute chart, etc.). It was proposed by Steve Shapiro one day after the market went against him literally almost before he had put the phone back into its cradle after placing an order. Like the rest of us, he too, has made decisions using emotion rather than logic more times than he cares to admit. Since we began applying it, the technique has saved both of us a great deal of money. There is more than one lesson in his explanation of what he calls his "Five Minute Rule", but what I like to call the "Shapiro Iteration."

The most difficult thing for any trader to do is isolate the emotional part of his thinking and keep it from interfering with his trading. One of the best ways to accomplish this task is to plan and place both the entry point and price objective before you make the trade.

Including both of these price points with a stop loss when you place your original order will reduce the emotional element of trading. The problem with this concept is that for whatever reason, most traders simply cannot operate this mechanically.

It is necessary, therefore, to be realistic and try to develop a safety valve that can protect us from ourselves if we cannot behave this rationally. The closest concept to a fail-safe rule I have found to use in the heat of trading is the "Shapiro Iteration" or "Five Minute Rule."

When a decision to put on a trade is made during market hours, it is often made on the basis of only one calculation, rather than the more reliable confirmation of a number of decisions drawing the same or similar conclusions about price.

Many times as we sit and watch the screen we experience the urge to make a trade because it is beginning to move in the direction we anticipated. We saw the trade before the move began, but for some reason did not put it on.

As the price moves our way, and particularly if it begins to accelerate, there is an emotional surge we experience that comes from a combination of being right about the trade, and feeling indecisive about not putting it on, as well as guilty/angry about losing the profit. It is precisely this eagerness to still want to "hop on the train before it gets too far from the station" that usually gets us in trouble. Unless the price action suddenly slows down drastically, or reverses altogether, the emotional surge will continue to swell and many times we will put on the trade, even though we logically know it is not the best course of action.

The result is too often what appears to be the vengeance of the trading gods. We have all had the experience of struggling with ourselves about placing such an order, and when we finally make the decision to do it, almost as soon as we put the phone back in the cradle the price action changes. We almost believe that the market was active and alive and just waiting for the exact moment we put on our one or two contracts to reverse the price movement.

It is especially important at these times to remember that when this happens, the market is not alive or right or wrong, and it is not punishing us for doing the wrong thing. The market simply and always *just is*. It is we who are right or wrong. It is we who punish ourselves for anger, or greed or indecision or not doing our homework.

After acting more times than I care to admit on this emotional impulse to place the right trade at the wrong time, a very simple conclusion presented itself. Because the time between actually putting on the trade and the time the market seemed to reverse was so small, (often it seemed to happen simultaneously no matter how hard I tried to "outsmart" or "beat" the market), the only logical way to deal with this seemingly insurmountable temptation was to write down the exact time and price when I finally decided to make the trade, and force myself to wait atleast five minutes, 300 seconds, before actually initiating it.

The logic was elegant in its simplicity. If the trading gods really were waiting in ambush for my emotions to drive me to make the trade at exactly the wrong moment, in five minutes I would observe a noticeable change in trend in the price action, proof that I should not have put on the trade.

When this is the case, the amount saved usually turns out to be substantial. This is true for two reasons. First, when the price reverses after a fast move in one direction, it is often an equally speedy and sizable retracement of the previous move. If I placed a close stop to limit the loss, it is usually hit rather quickly. If a stop was not put on, it became a destructive game of playing catch up and possibly letting a small loss that should not have occurred in the first place develop into a larger loss. When this happens your focus usually follows the loss instead of looking for another profitable situation.

If in fact the trade still looked good five minutes after my emotions told me I couldn't wait a minute longer, then all I did was lose a little of the profit that was still to be made. In either case the net is still a gain.

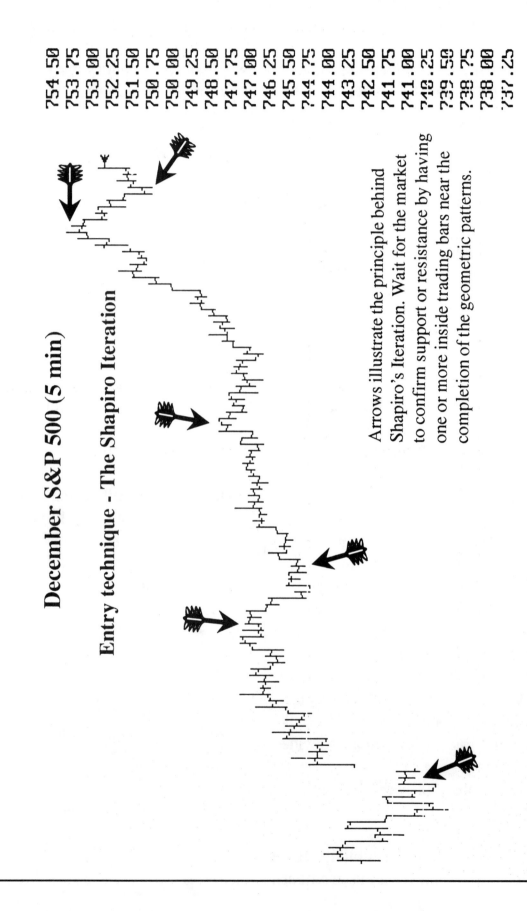

Fibonacci Ratios with Pattern Recognition

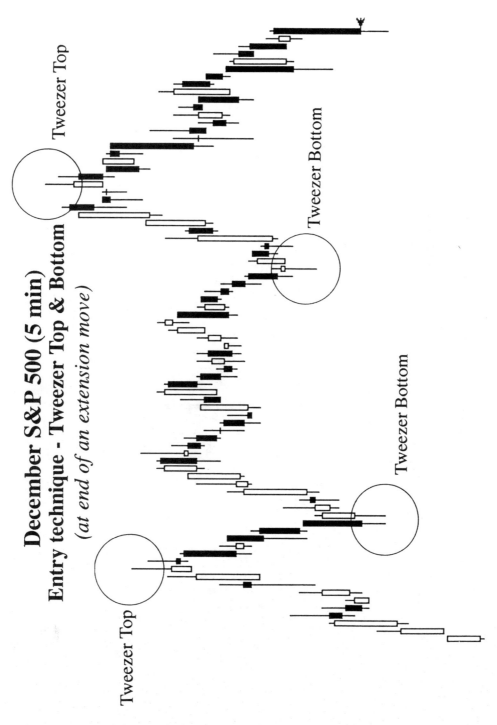

December S&P 500 (5 min)
Entry technique - Tweezer Top & Bottom
(at end of an extension move)

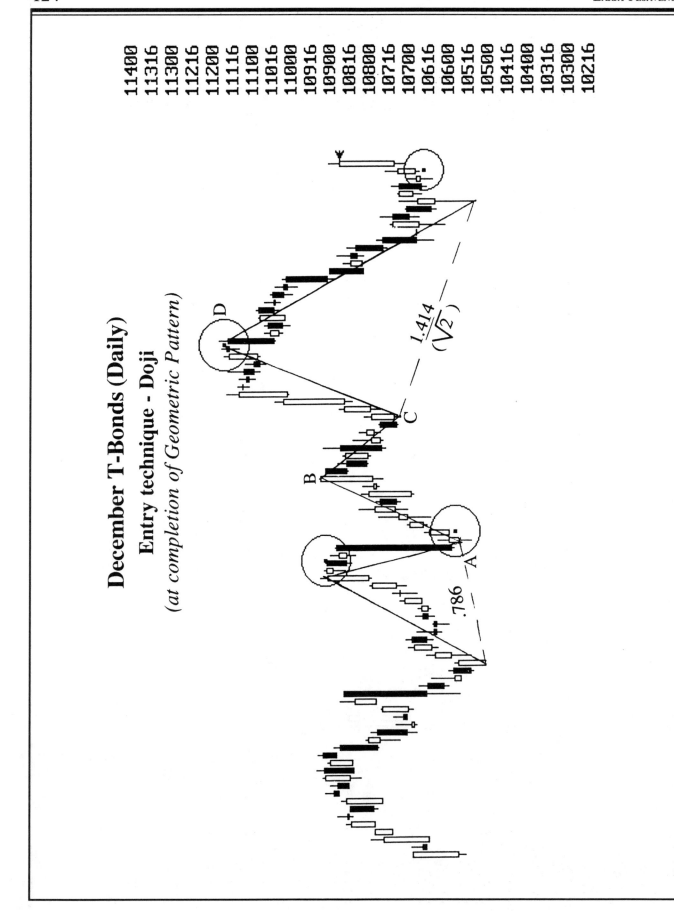

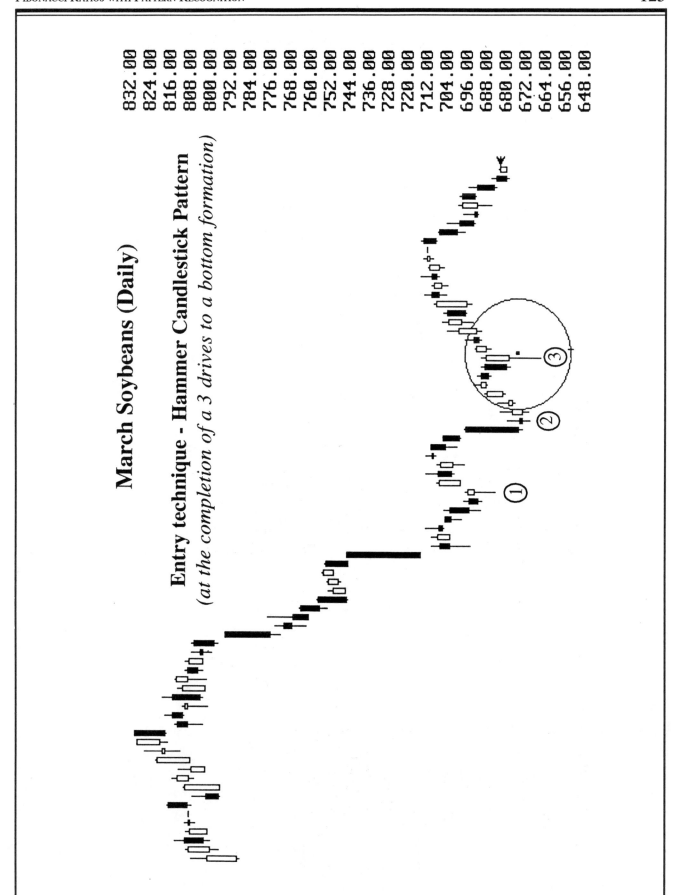

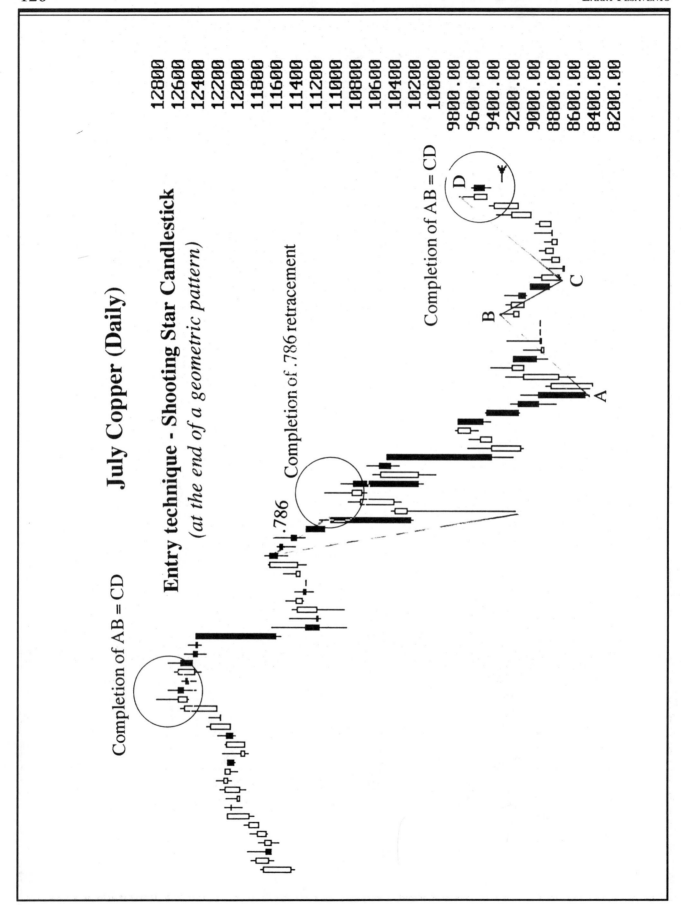

APPENDIX I

TRADING RECORD
TRADE PLANNING SHEET

Date	Commodity	Pattern	Entry	Exit	Stop Protection	Profit/Loss

Stop protection should be no more than 3 percent of total trading equity.

APPENDIX II

DESCRIPTION OF GARTLEY "222"

This is the description of the Gartley "222" pattern exactly as it appears on pages 221 and 222 of his book, *Profits in the Stock Market*.

One of the Best Trading Opportunities

In the life of those who dabble on Wall street, at some time or another there comes a yearning--- "just to buy them right, once, if never again." For those who have patience, the study of top and bottom patterns will provide such an opportunity every now and then--the chance does not arise everyday, but when it does, a worthwhile opportunity, with small risk becomes available.

Figure 27 - A

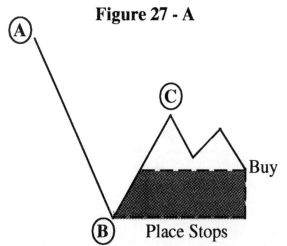

Let us look at Figure 27(A). When, after an intermediate decline in either a bull or a bear market, such as A-B in the diagram, has proceeded for some time, and activity has shown a definite tendency to dry up, indication that liquidation is terminating, a minor rally like B-C sets in, with volume expanding on the upside. And when a minor decline, after cancelling a third to a half of the preceding minor advance (B-C) comes to a halt, with volume drying up again, a real opportunity is presented to buy stocks, with a stop under the previous low.

In eight out of ten cases wherein each of these specific conditions occurs, a rally, which will provide a worthwhile profit, ensues. In the other two cases, only small losses have to be taken. In trading this formation, the observer is depending upon the probability that either a head-and-shoulders, or double bottom, which are the two reversal patterns which occur most frequently, is developing.

The art in conducting an operation of this kind lies in:

a. Having the patience to wait until a decline of substantial proportions has developed;

b. Observing that all conditions laid down are present;

c. Having the courage to buy just as soon as the minor reaction which tests the bottom shows signs of terminating; and

d. Having the courage to get out with a fair profit (10-20 per cent), or at least protect it with stops.

Hourly charts of the averages, available for guiding the operation, repay the market student for all the efforts he puts into keeping them day after day, when they are of less practical use.

Similar opportunities occasionally develop for that small part of the trading fraternity that the intestinal fortitude and temperament to sell stocks short. The case in reverse is laid out in of Figure 27(B).

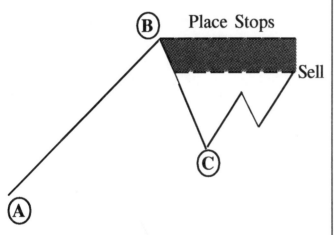

Figure 27 (B)

Gartley's book was written in the 1930's and things have changed dramatically about the markets. Not the markets themselves, but the way they are reported. Communication is now instantaneous because of the statellite dishes around the world connected to all the computer trading desks around the world. During Gartley's era, the Western Union tickertape was the method of communciation. As I wrote that last sentence, I realized that is how I learned to trade soybeans with Dave Nelson on his Trans Lux ticker tape.

Thousands of new stocks and commodity markets have been introduced since Gartley's time. Most of these are very liquid and easy to gain access to the chart patterns. This is particularly true for the intraday charts. In this section of the appendix, I have selected some intraday charts illustrating these patterns.

Included in the appendix is the page on my monitor that shows what commoditites and stocks I follow. Each has a monthly, daily and intraday chart pattern. Intraday charts are 2 minutes, 5 minutes, 30 minutes, 60 minutes as well as a tick chart to record every tick. This is helpful to gauge whether or not you are filled on your order and at what price.

As one reads the "222" pattern described by H. M. Gartley, three basic virtues are suggested for trading.

1) Patience to wait for the market formation to develop.

2) Courage to put the order in and a protective stop to minimize risk.

3) Fortitude and temperament to sell short. Again protecting the positions with stops.

The "222" is one of the best patterns a trader can expect. When it does not work it usually means that a greater trend continuation is in progress. Failure of the "222" pattern can be anticipated in several ways:

1. The presence of a huge gap near the D termination point.

2. Wide range price ranges as point D is forming.

3. After the formation of point D the market fails to reverse. This may indicate a level of consolidation before resuming the trend.

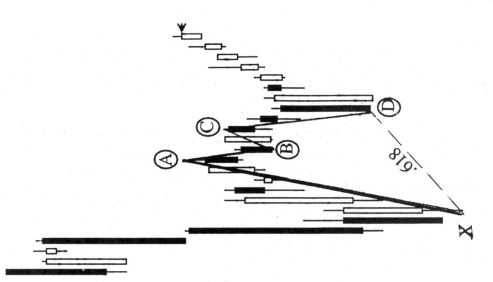

GARTLEY "222" CHARTS
March S&P 500 (5 min)

Interpretation of the Gartley "222" Pattern

This is not a "222" pattern in the classical Gartley interpretation. The reason lies in the B-C swing for 2 reasons:

1. Not enough time is contained in the B-C swing. It should be at least 5 time bars.
2. The B-C swing should be a .618 of A-B.

Finally, the CD move has extended way beyond the 1.618 of B-C.

March Swiss Franc (5 min)

Failure of the Gartley "222" Pattern

This was a perfect "222" pattern. All ratios were present and symmetrical. The trade did not work. Trend was still down. The risk was very small compared to the profit potential. Protective stop placed below point D.

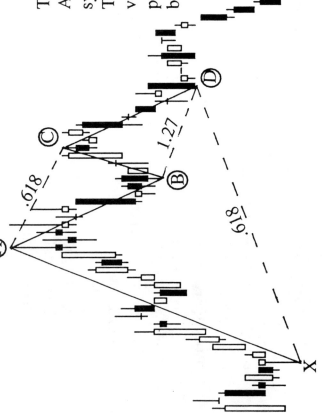

Fibonacci Ratios with Pattern Recognition

March S&P 500 (1 min)

Gartley "222" Pattern

This is a 1 minute S&P chart illustrating the "222" pattern. It can be used as an entry technique. I do not recommend trading of a 1 minute chart! What is important is to recognize the "222" on any time frame. On this particular day (Jan 4, 1997) the S&P 500 went 16 points down the reversed, closing up (a 36 point intraday swing).

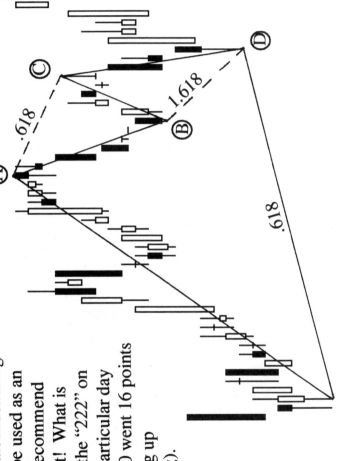

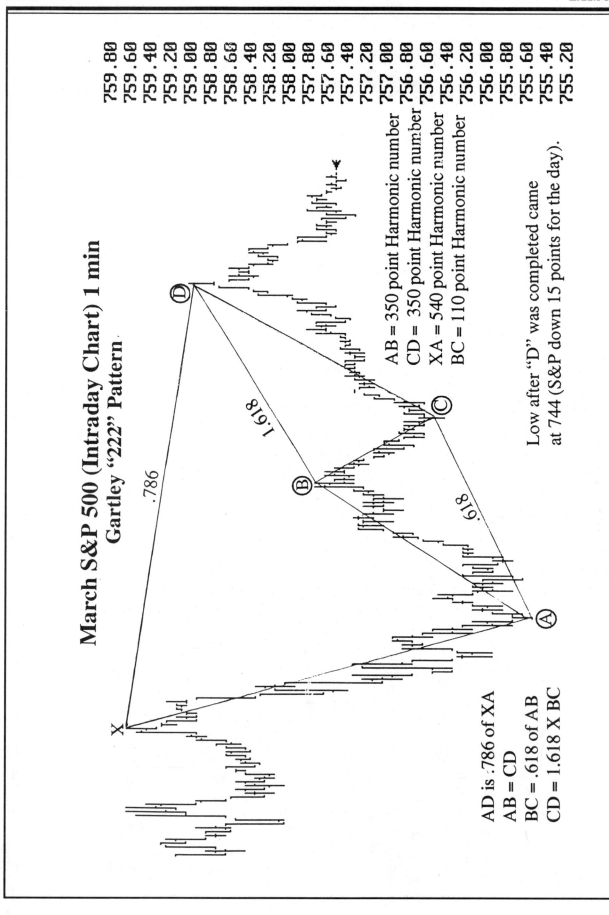

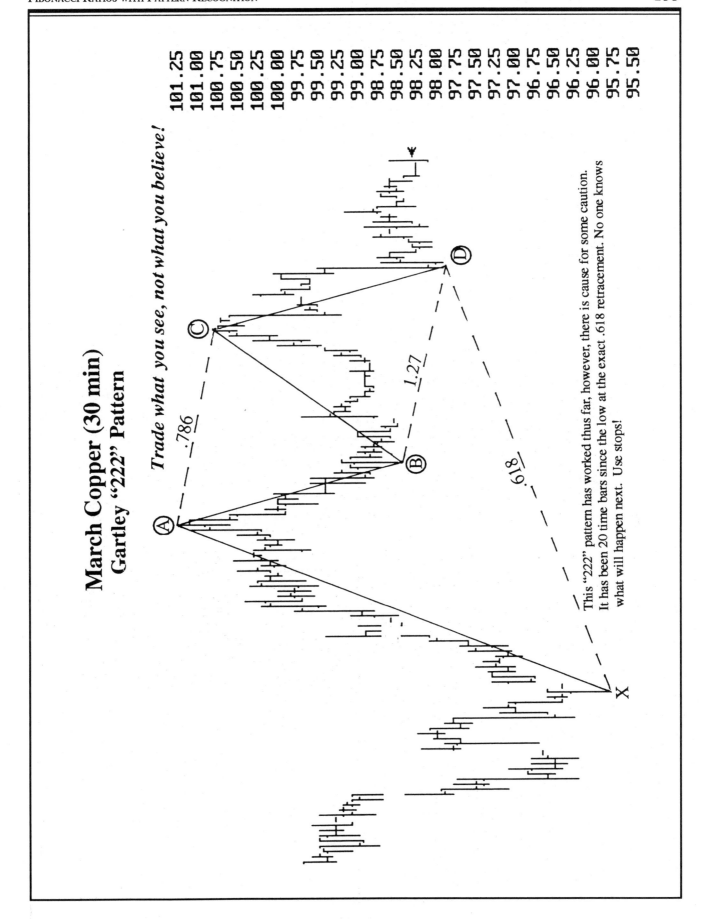

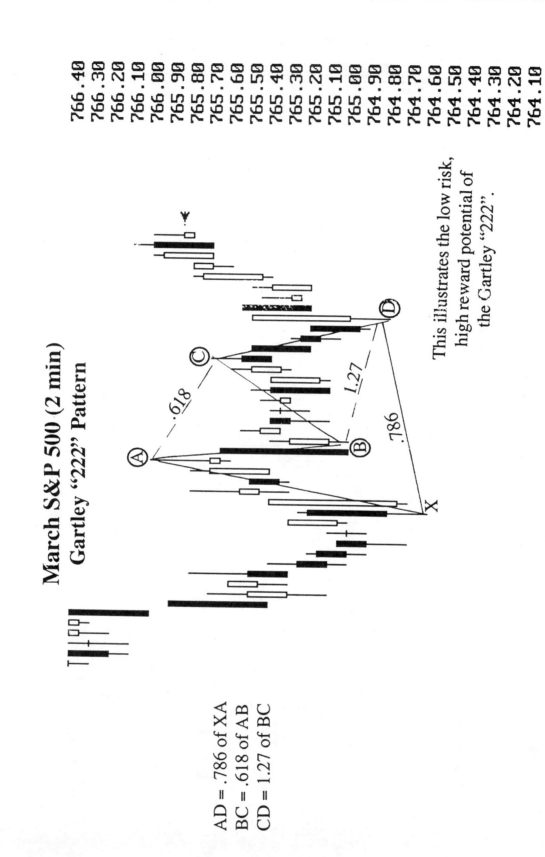

Fibonacci Ratios with Pattern Recognition

March S&P 500 (5 min)
Gartley "222" Pattern

X = Opening price

X-A = 270 Harmonic number
A-D = 170 Harmonic number
AB = CD
BC = .786 of AB
CD = 1.27 of BC
AD = .618 of XA

This "222" was further enhanced by the fact that the sell signal at "D" was below the opening price.

You should be trading below the opening price which should be the high of the day more than 80% of the time.
(See opening price chapter.)

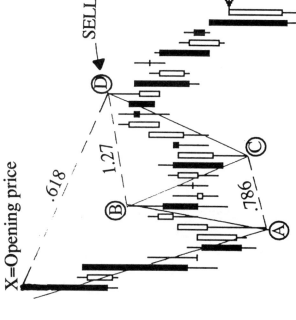

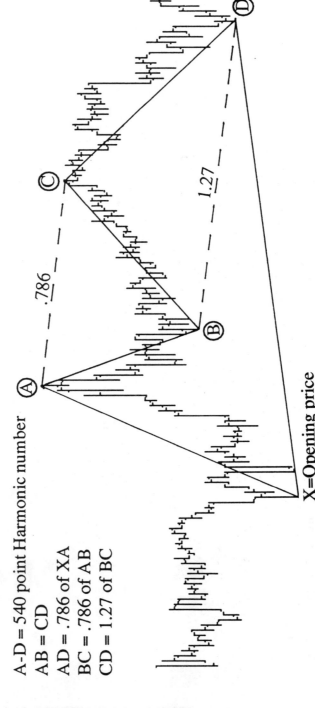

March S&P 500 (5 min)

Gartley "222" Pattern

A-D = 540 point Harmonic number
AB = CD
AD = .786 of XA
BC = .786 of AB
CD = 1.27 of BC

X=Opening price

This "222" was found by retracing .786 of the early daily range above the opening price.
Remember: buy above opening price or sell below opening price.

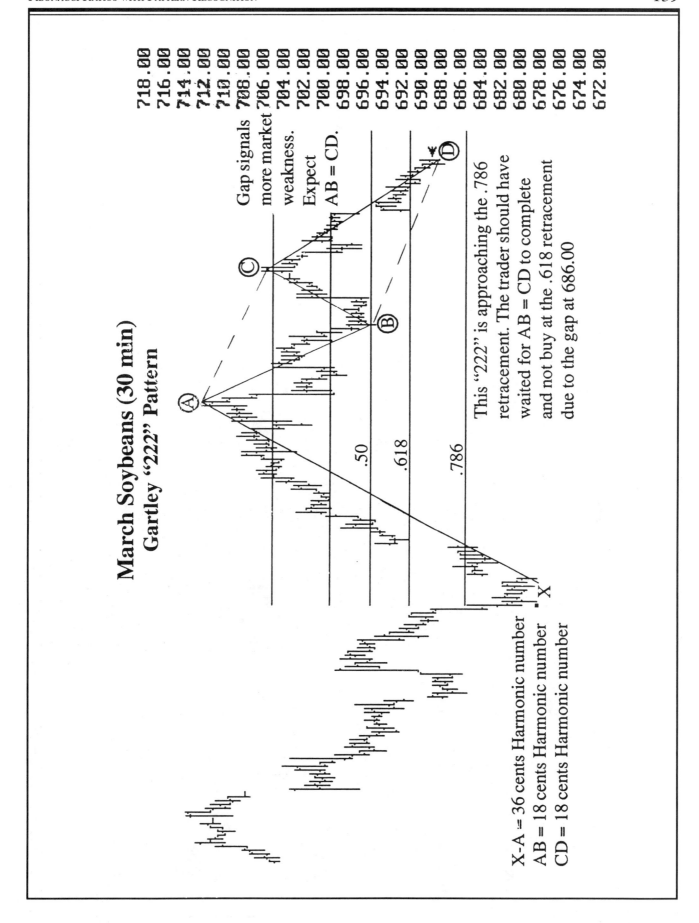

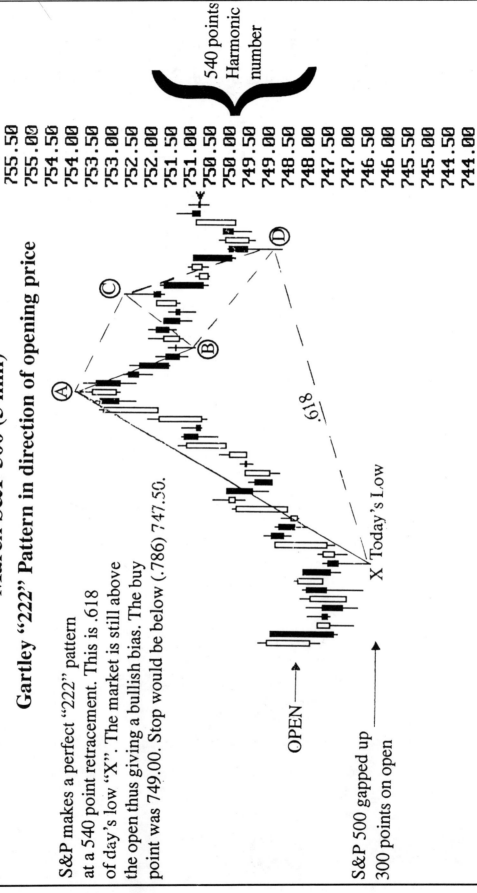

March S&P 500 (5 min)
Gartley "222" Pattern in direction of opening price

S&P makes a perfect "222" pattern at a 540 point retracement. This is .618 of day's low "X". The market is still above the open thus giving a bullish bias. The buy point was 749.00. Stop would be below (.786) 747.50.

S&P 500 gapped up 300 points on open

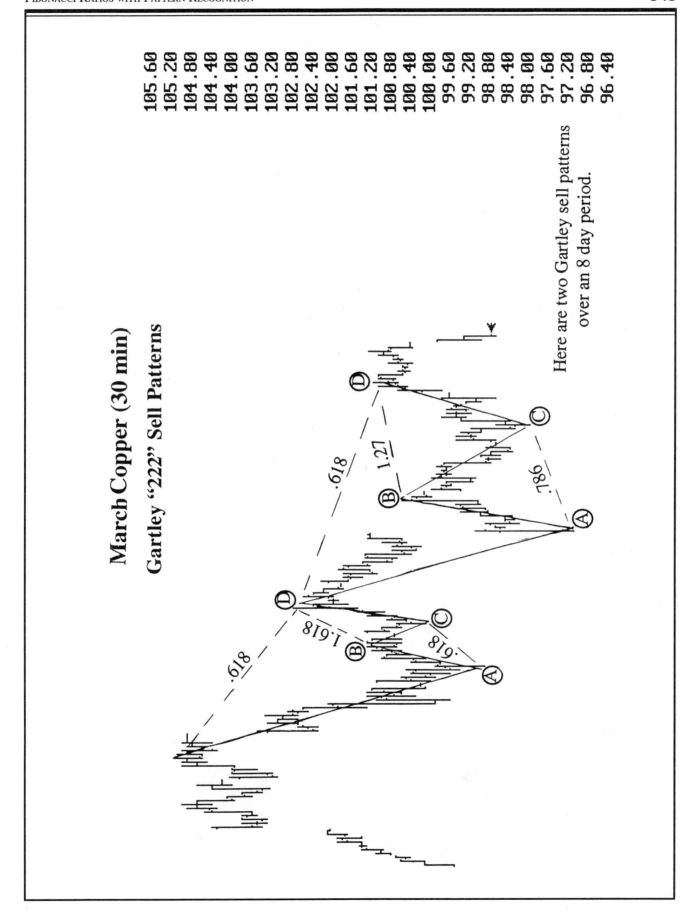

APPENDIX II-B

Know why this is not a Gartley "222" pattern.

Dow Jones Industrials (5 min)

The key to why this is not a "222" pattern lies in the BC move. It was not at either the .618 or .786 retracement levels. The fact that the market could not rally from point B to point C was indicating that a .618 or .786 retracement was developing.

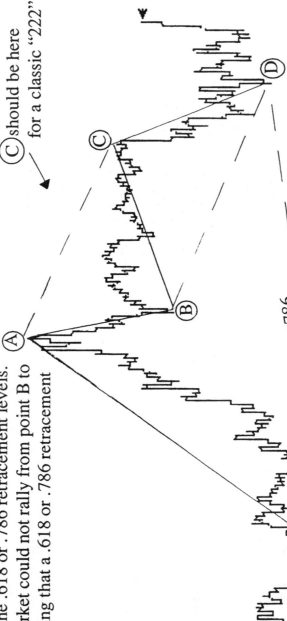

THIS IS NOT A GARTLEY "222" PATTERN

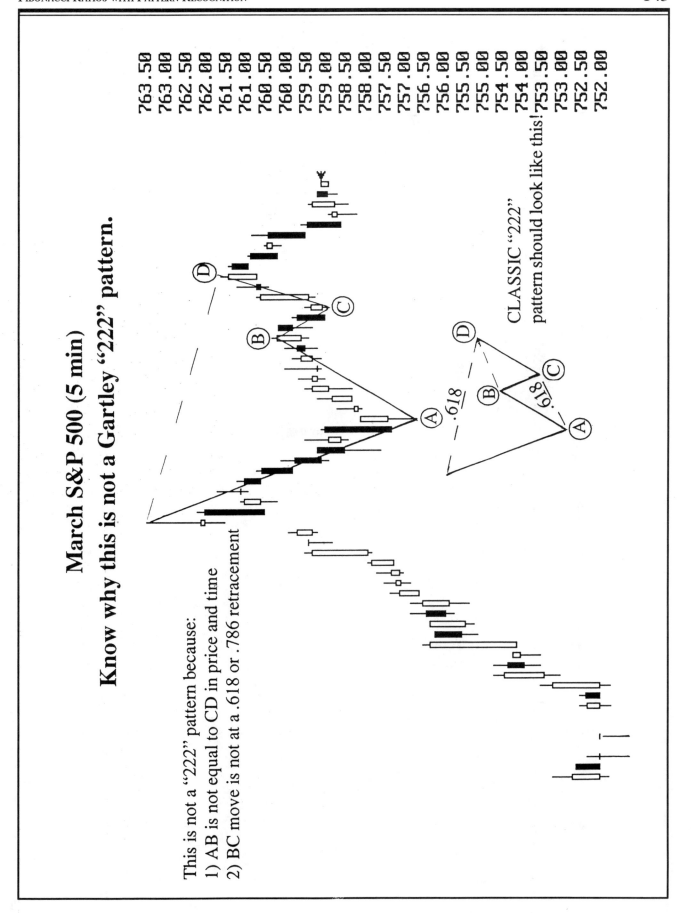

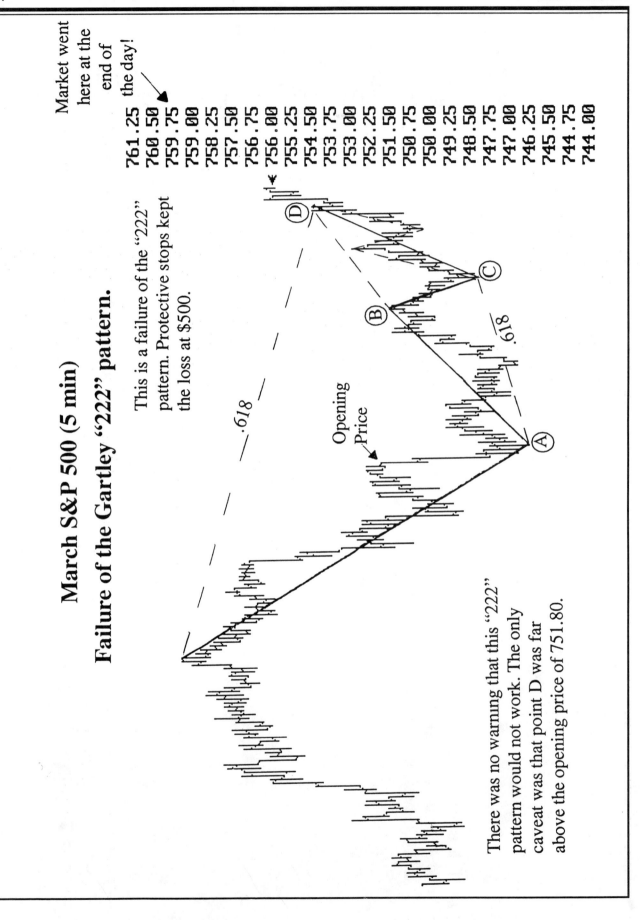

Fibonacci Ratios with Pattern Recognition

March 1997 Copper (30 min)
Failure of the Gartley "222" pattern.

Prices ended the day above $105.00/lb.

Price Gap

Here is an example of a failure of a "222" pattern. Selling at "D" was the correct move but it only worked for 1 day and about $500. The big price gap on the following day was an indication that the market was going to continue higher. This would have been a very small loss. (*Under $200*)

Point C is also a "222" buy point!

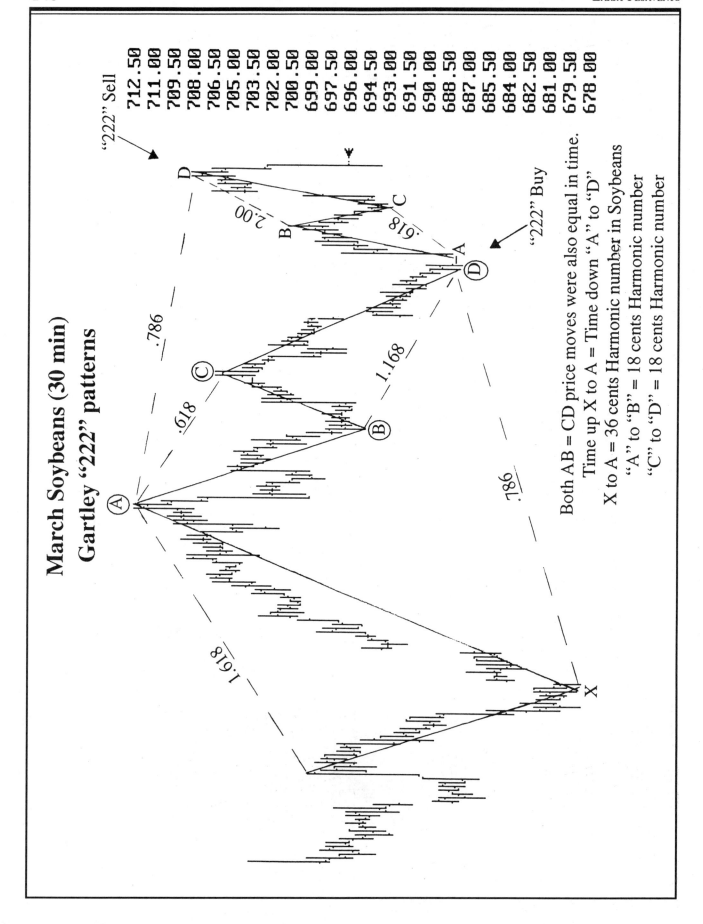

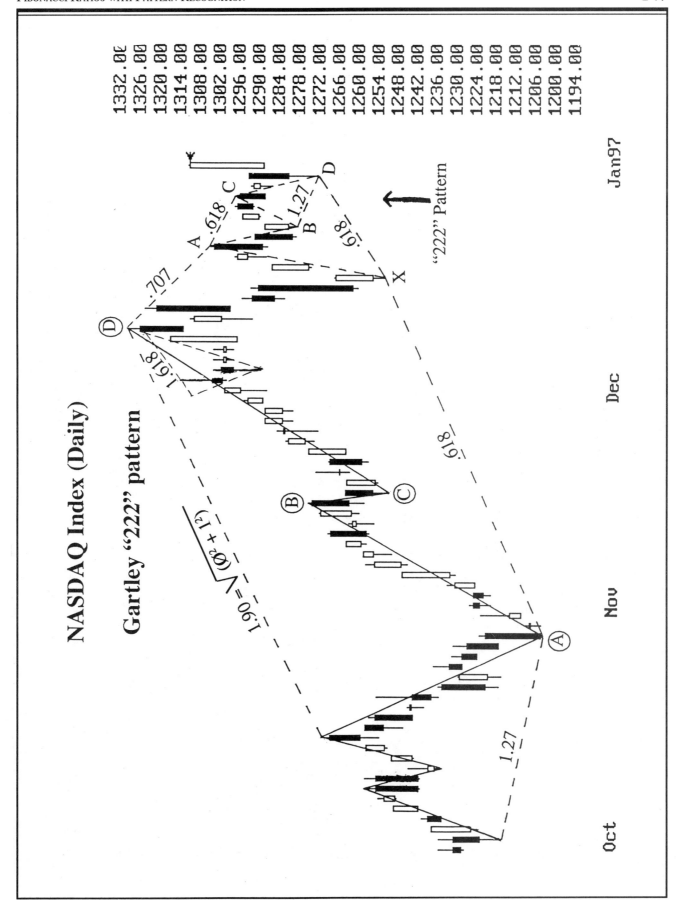

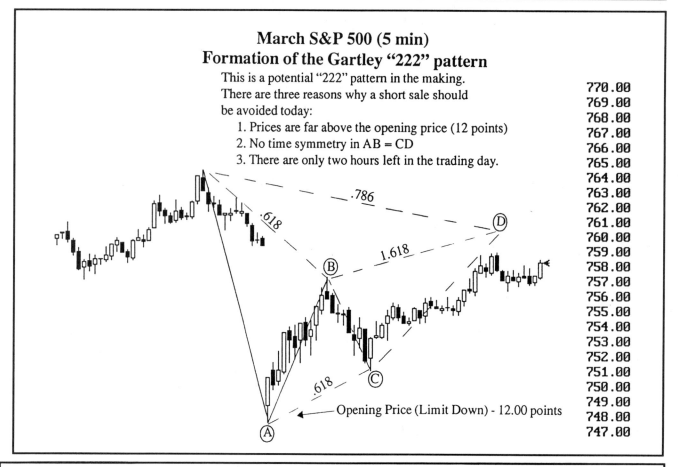

March S&P 500 (5 min)
Formation of the Gartley "222" pattern

This is a potential "222" pattern in the making.
There are three reasons why a short sale should
be avoided today:
  1. Prices are far above the opening price (12 points)
  2. No time symmetry in AB = CD
  3. There are only two hours left in the trading day.

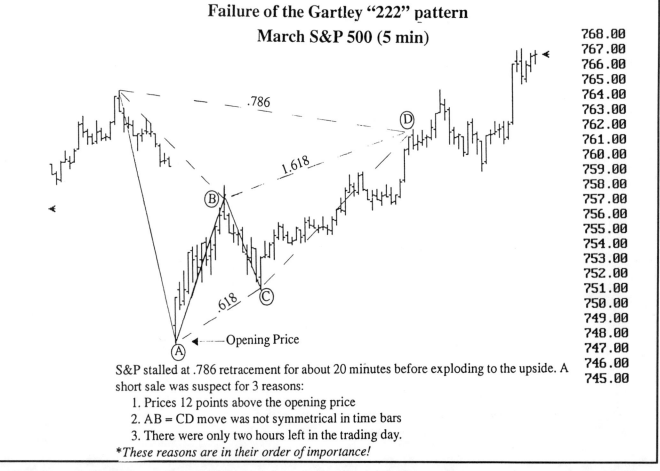

Failure of the Gartley "222" pattern
March S&P 500 (5 min)

S&P stalled at .786 retracement for about 20 minutes before exploding to the upside. A short sale was suspect for 3 reasons:
  1. Prices 12 points above the opening price
  2. AB = CD move was not symmetrical in time bars
  3. There were only two hours left in the trading day.

These reasons are in their order of importance!

APPENDIX III

PORTFOLIO PAGE

This is the portfolio page I use each day. From these speculative vehicles I search for the various patterns.

* The Transportation, Cash S&P, and Tick Indices are used as confirmations of the patterns. The same patterns are present in the cash indices.

DESCRIPTION	SYMBOL	LAST	NET	HIGH	LOW	OPEN
US Bonds	US7H	11401	+3	11406	11331	11331
Swiss Francs	SF7H	.7454	-.0011	.7479	.7439	.7461
Deutsche Mark	DM7H	.6452	-.0012	.6473	.6450	.6469
Wheat	W7H	386.50	-3.00	389.00	385.25	388.75
Jap Yen	JY7H	.8712	-.0038	.8730	.8695	.8728
S&P 500	SP7H	764.90	+0.30	767.00	764.60	764.60
Dow	INDU	6565.90	+4.99	6576.28	6560.91	6560.91
Soybean Meal	SM7H	220.50	-1.30	220.50	218.70	220.40
Soybean	S7F	700.00	-1.50	700.00	698.50	699.50
Corn	C7H	262.50	-2.00	263.00	262.25	263.00
Gold	GC7G	371.10	+0.00	371.70	371.00	371.20
Silver	SI7H	482.00	-9.30	492.00	480.00	490.50
Transport	TRAN	2286.03	-1.66	2288.61	2286.03	2287.69
TICK Index	TICK	140.00		565.00	127.00	127.00
Copper	HG7H	99.00	+0.40	99.15	98.10	98.00
NYFE	YX7H	401.85	+0.40	402.90	401.80	402.60
Cash S&P	SPY	757.95	+1.16	759.20	756.79	
Crude Oil	CL7G	25.51	+0.29	25.55	25.13	25.40
Soybean Oil	BO7H	.2339	+.0009	.2340	.2339	.2340
Natural Gas	NR7H	27.80	-2.04	28.00	27.50	27.70

APPENDIX IV

ROOTS AND UPROOTS

The first thing I was ever told about Larry Pesavento was that he traded stocks using the stars. Being a self proclaimed pseudo-intellectual liberal from the East newly arrived in a small central coast California town, I immediately pictured a wizened old guy with a long white beard who wore a large, black pointed hat and cloak, both covered with white glistening stars and half moons. Maybe he even walked around carrying a large staff and tapped it on the ground for support as he walked.

At the time, I recently came west to accept a teaching position at California Polytechnic State University (Cal Poly) and was still in the process of meeting people. One of them was Michael Weintraub, the gregarious owner of a store that sells excellent fur and leather goods in San Louis Obispo. This, in a small town where the mean annual temperature was 70.2 degrees. The paradox was amazing to me and so was Michael. He likes to shock people and when he asked me what I liked to do in my spare time and I mentioned traded commodities, he melodramatically told me about Larry.

When I met Larry in Michael's store on night after hearing about him, I was startled by his appearance. I was almost disappointed there was no pointed cap, no cloak, no stars or half moons. At first glance he looked just like everybody else, until you noticed the constant twinkle in his eye that spoke of living life, loving it and inviting the observer to share the ride. No magic, no mystery. Just a nice guy who liked people/ He appeared to be generous and giving. And he was.

Don't be fooled by appearance was the first lesson I learned for LP. (As our friendship grew he came to call me "Doc" and I would call him LP.) The moral here is: watch your expectations. Better yet, don't have them and they won't be violated. With respect to the markets, don't look for something you want to be there. Learn to see what the market offers and respect what's there. Put more succinctly, don't look for what you WANT to be in a trade, learn to see what there IS in the trade. This was a lesson that would haunt us both.

When Michael introduced us, he said to me, "Go ahead, ask him anything you want," as if to imply Larry possessed some kind of secret monopoly on the wisdom of markets.

LP looked at Michael, who he knew loved "to stir the pot." To reduce my awkwardness and embarrassment at Michael's intentioned boldness Larry just smiled his disarming smile and said, "Go ahead, I don't' mind. I love what I do and love to talk about the market."

That began both my friendship with LP and a series of discussions that not only covered the mechanics of trading, but virtually every aspect of life and how it related to the psychology of trading and trading as a metaphor for life.

Soon after we met, LP invited me to his trading room to continue our discussions and watch him trade. Being a late night person at the time, there were few things I was willing to get up to see at 5:20 AM. Bonds and currencies start trading at that time on the West coast (8:20 AM NY time). LP seemed so interesting and funny that I thought I would give it a try. It was one of the wisest decisions I ever made. We would sit and watch the markets and LP would tell me market "war stories" about his days as a stockbroker and floor trader, and what he thought was going to happen that day. I was delighted at how much he knew and how funny he could be and how often he was right about the markets.

Larry is the best pure trader I ever met or read about. One morning on a particularly slow trading day he turned to me and said, "I'm bored. Let's paper trade some bellies." Larry loves to trade pork bellies and has an incredible knack for it. In a short time he made 15 straight profitable paper trades. On the basis of just one contract he literally could have made more than 1000% that day trading one contract.

When he would say, "Let's put one on now," or "Let's get out of it now," I would invariably ask, "Why did you do that?" He would invariably reply, "Because it was the right thing to do." "Come on. LP, could you be a little more specific," I would say, feigning a mock annoyance with his cavalier attitude. He would look at me with exaggerated exasperation and tease, "Come on Doc, are you kidding me? This is easy. By now you should not only know this, but be able to teach it." Then, of course, he would tell me, slowly and carefully, always emphasizing the importance of never putting on a trade without a stop, and equally important, the value of knowing when to get out.

It didn't take long to see he was right. It was easier than I thought once I began to see the patterns. It really doesn't take long to learn them and be able to pick them out on any chart just by looking. The techniques in this book work, but what doesn't necessarily accompany that knowledge is the wisdom to apply it properly.

When I first started watching LP trade I asked what I thought was a logical question, one that I since heard many times. "Does it work for everything, and how do you know?" When I first asked, LP just smiled and grabbed a chart. He cut off the name and the scale so I didn't know what it was, whether it was a stock or commodity, or what the time bars were. He gave me the chart and told me to look for the patterns. "But there are no time bars on it. How will I know what I'm looking at?" I protested, without thinking my objection through.

For a rare moment he was serious. "Pay attention. Stop looking for what you WANT to see. Just look at what's there and what you DO see."

Of course he was right. Once I stopped looking for what I expected and started looking at what was there, the patterns just jumped out at me. He saw my face change and slipped back into the non-serious LP.

A case in point. One morning we were watching the market and LP was on the phone. The conversation did not go well and when LP put the receiver in the cradle he immediately picked it back up, dialed his broker and put on a very bad trade with no stop, which immediately started going against him. He watched the price go against him and ignored a number of other possibilities we were considering as he let his frustration and annoyance with himself grow.

After a few minutes of watching him stew, I turned to him and quietly, "LP do you know what you just did?"

He looked at me like he had just come out of a trance. He knew exactly what I meant and true professional that he is, said, "Doc, you're right. That was really dumb. I let myself get emotional." He immediatley dialed his broker and closed the trade with a small loss. Always the friend and teacher, he said without embarassment, "Let's talk about what just happened."

We identified a number of lessons to be learned from the actions of those few minutes. First, when you trade, try to think of nothing else at the time. Focus on what you are doing, how you are doing it, and most important of all, why you are doing it. The market is what it is, and does what it does. It doesn't care about who we are or what we do. If we choose to act on bad a decision, it's okay with the market. How many times have all of us heard someone complain, "Look at what the market did to me today?" The market did NOTHING to that individual or anybody else. It doesn't know that he's alive. Or care. It owes him or us nothing. It simply is. What happened he did to himself. The successful trader makes bad decisions based on the probabilities that the inherent harmony of the markets will repeat itself, i.e. what has happened before it will happen again. The trader's analysis suggests when, where, and to what extent. The patterns that evolve are always similiar but seldom the same. They may be thought of as the grammar of how the market speaks, in the same way how words relate are the building blocks of language.

The second lesson is to keep your emotions out of your trading. Mathematics is clear, concise and logical. The pattern recognition and trend analysis in this book provide techniques to put the probabilities in your favor, but you must be in the proper frame of mind to use them profitably. Outside concerns, especially personal or emotional ones, must be put aside (admittedly difficult to do), or you must not trade. To allow "things" to bother you when you are trying to trade is almost a guaranteed prescription for disaster. The value of having the wisdom and the discipline to see the difference and act on it properly cannot be over calculated. The money you DON'T lose because of poor judgement and emotionally driven decisions can be far greater and more important to you that the profits you do make by exercising proper trading technique. The emotional price of making a bad decision based on emotion can be more costly and psychologically more damaging that the loss of money. Money can be remade more easily than confidence and self assurance can be restored. Fortunately in this case Larry caught himself going in a dangerous direction on that trade and was disciplined enough to cut his loss and move on.

The third lesson is that making a bad decision and staying with it when you know it's wrong, keeps you from aeeking and taking advantage of other profitable opportunities. A trade, especially a bad one, is over when it's over. Forget it and move on.

These observations seem cold and calculating. And difficult to implement. They are, all of the above. They are also how a professioanl trader trades. They require discipline and confidence and the ego strength to take responsibilty for our actions. Whenever LP and I followed our guidelines we invariably make money. When we thought we were smarter than the market or "just wanted a little more," the opposite was just as certain.

One of the best examples of this concept that became a running joke with us is the story about how "Ten dimes make a dollar." One day, when LP had just concluded a very profitable run of trades, he seemed to linger over his decision about when to exit the last trade. It earned a substantial profit very quickly and LP was hesitant about exiting it. Soon after it reached the profit point LP had projected, and gone a little farther, the price changed direction and a fairly large profit turned into a loss.

"LP, why did you let that happen?" I asked.

Somewhat sheepishly, he replied, "I just made a lot of money hitting singles and doubles, I felt like trying for a home run."

"Aw c'mon LP," I chided him with a smile, you know better than that. Every time either one of us does that we get nailed." We both knew better, but every once in a while we both still did it.

When he sets his mind to it, Larry can be almost a perfect trader, doing exactly everything how he teaches it. It is important to realize that doesn't mean always making a profit. What it does mean is that doing the right thing for the right reason at the right time will make a net profit over time, quite possibly a large one. You learn to look at the net results of ten trades, or twenty, not just one.

"Doc, stop picking on me. I know what I did," he laughed.

What I said next just came out. I didn't think about until after I said it and we both laughed. "LP, ten dimes make a dollar. You want a dollar, don't be lazy. Make ten dimes, 'cause a dollar might not be there in one gulp."

Larry kept a straight face as he stopped, looked thoughtful, reached for a pencil and made a big show of writing as he spoke the words,"Wait, Doc, I'm a little slow, let me write this down, 'Ten ... dimes...make ... a dollar ...'"

We both laughed and talked about it. The many morals were clear, and we both were guilty of violating our guidelines too many times. Don't be greedy; don't look for what's not there; take what the market gives; don't think that after you make a profit you're trading with the market's money. Once you make it, it's yours. Don't give it back foolishly. Carefully plan every trade you make. Think of it as the most important trade you ever made -- until the next one.

Larry was right about how easy it becomes to recognize and spot the patterns and eventually I did begin to help him teach his technique. Like college teaching, helping LP train commodity traders usually taught me as much or more as I might teach them. Seeing the light of knowledge suddenly appear on someone's face where a split second before there was uncertainty, is not only psychologically rewarding for the teacher, but also offers the opportunity to analyze when the light dawned and why. That provides insight into the workings of the student's mind as well as the teacher's. Both LP and I learned much from our students. As with the market, the secret was to observe and see what was there, not what we wanted to be there.

When I observed that teaching how to trade the markets was pretty much the same as teaching communication at the university, LP just smiled that boyish smile of his and asked in exaggerated wonder, "You're surprised!?" The truth was that learning about the markets taught me more about my behavior and that of others than anything else. Again, LP and I talked about this process many times. It taught us both how to "see" many things more clearly. As LP taught me, the market was indeed a metaphor for a great deal more.

Perhaps the best examples of this process occurred a number of times with beginning students who just learned to trade.

Larry would instruct him to choose three or four different markets and pick one commodity from each to trade. When asked, we usually suggested bonds, a metal and a grain.

After three months or so, students would call back to tell us how their trading was going. Often when students called, they would report 30% or 40% profits for the period. Then they would ask if it was time to start trading three or four more commodities. This question always made us laugh because we knew what was coming next. We would respond with our own question, "What would happen if instead of doubling the number of COMMODITIES you traded, you doubled the number of CONTRACTS you traded? Assuming everything continued about the same, how would you change your percentage of profit?

Most of the time the student would take a moment to do some math and generally answer, "I'm not sure." This would cause us to laugh again and purposely irritate the student. "Why are you laughing?" would be the next question.

"You're not listening," one of us would say. "The PERCENTAGE of profit would stay the same. The AMOUNT of profit would change. Why increase your amount of work (the number of commodities you trade and therefore have to analyze) when all you have to do to make more money is increase the number of CONTRACTS? To quote the old clich, ' if it ain't broke, don't fix it.' Don't make more work for yourself, just more money."

The other example occured when a student would call and say "I just made ten ticks in bonds" or "I just made 5 cents in beans, what should I do? Should I close the trade or wait and maybe get some more?"

Again we would laugh, and again, the student would at first grow annoyed with our laughter. One of us would ask how long the trade took to happen. The answer was usually, "half an hour" or "an hour." We would laugh again and one of us would ask, "Is that what you were looking for from this trade? In response to a "yes," we would continue, "would you prefer the trade took four hours to make a profit? If you have a chance to make what your analysis suggested what was there, take it and look for another trade. Would you rather get your ten ticks in half an hour or half a day?" What usually clinched it, was when we asked "If we told you before the market opened how to make ten ticks today, would you do it and be satisfied?"

If the answer was "yes," as it usually was, we would tell the student to answer his own question about what to do regarding the trade. It was an important part of the teaching of the teaching process for the student to be satisfied with his own decision, not just ours. That helped develop a student's confidence in trading.

Often a student defended the original decision and its result by adding, "But I thought . . ." One of us would interrupt at that point and gently say, "No, you didn't think, and that is what will cost you money. Now what did you learn today?" The student would respond that he was at first annoyed by our laughter, and didn't think the situation through. That is precisely the effect we wanted. It was unlikely in the extreme that the student would make that mistake again. We all want to be right as much as we want to make a profit. Sometimes more so. And that's where the trouble begins. An accurate analysis and proper entry can be easily ruined by an emotional response that changes the rules. Good technique, but bad psychology equal a bad result. Students usually saw the lesson, laughed with us about their first reaction, thanked us and said goodbye. They called us to ask about a specific trade, but we would try to turn it into a lesson and get them to answer their own question. It usually worked. It was the equivalent of that old parable that teaches, when you give a starving man a fish, he will eat for one day. If you give him a fishing line and teach him how to fish, he will eat every day.

When they called back a few months after that, we shared another laugh when they told us their percentages stayed the same, but they were making more money and still making mistakes, but not THAT one.

We once had a student who wanted very much to learn to trade the S&P profitably. As we showed him what to do, he kept saying, "I understand what you're telling me, but I don't do it that way."

Finally one of us asked if he was making a profit trading. "Not really," he replied. Our experience taught us he really meant he was losing his shirt.

Then maybe you should try it another way," we suggested. When he left he was still doing it his way.

Finally one of us asked him if he was making a profit trading. "Not really," he replied. Our experience taught us he really meant he was losing his shirt.

The anecdote illustrates the proper answer to a very important question. "Would you rather be right, or get what you want?"

The reader is left to decide.

This story also illustrates another point -- it is only at the beginning of discovery that we realize how great our ignorance. To this end, Larry is fond of quoting a Confucian proverb: When the student is ready, the teacher will appear.

A spiritual friend of ours once told me, "Go beyond the boundary of yourself to know..." The technique taught in this book allows the serious student to do exactly that.

Over the years of my college teaching, increasing numbers of my students constantly complained about almost everything and almost everyone. They saw themselves as victims. Nothing was ever their fault. They were jailhouse lawyers who would argue for everything extra they could get, whether or not they earned it. They represent the direction much of society is taking today. Too many people refuse to take responsibility for their own actions because they see themselves as victims of unseen malevolent forces. They become the traders who say, "Look what the market did to me today."

When these students would argue for a few more points they really didn't deserve, I used to tell them, "Let me think about it. After I make up my mind, I will listen to reason, for then it can do no good." Or smile mischieviously, and tell them, "Sometimes you're the bug and sometimes you're the windshield."

Flip retorts or positive affirmations are helpful and sometimes even fun, but they will never substitute for knowledge, confidence, and personal responsibility. Ernest Hemingway once wrote, "Every man has fears; those who face them with dignity also have courage."

That is the bottom line. The inevitable destiny of ignorance and mistake of arrogance is failure and self pity.

Remember, Babe Ruth hit 714 runs, but he also struck out 1330 times.

APPENDIX V

SOME PRACTICAL TIPS ON CYCLES

Cycles are a funny lot---
Totally random they are not---
Just when you think you have a great find---
Along comes another to challenge your mind.

                ----S.W.S.

The above poem sums up the study of cycles. I believe that speculation markets are non-random and chaotic. Within this chaos are respectable patterns of price and time. My Tomahawk neural network program has shown this to be true on a very consistent basis. There are two cycle principles that I think each trader should explore. These were first brought to my attention when I studied Jim Hurst's Cyclicic material in 1971. The first principle is that of high translation. This means that bearish and bullish cycles have distinct characteristics.

Bullish Cycle - High Translation to Right

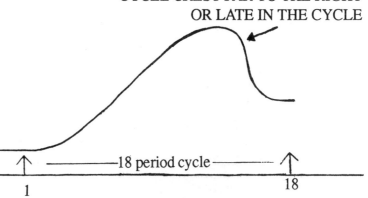

Bullish markets spend more time going up.

Bearish Cycle -- High Translation to Left

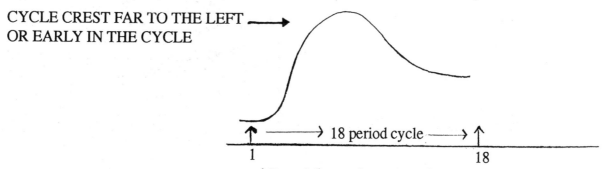

Bearish markets spend more time going down.

The second cycle principle is that of nominality. Cycles usually repeat in equal increments. For instance, if there is a 9 period cycle it will usually repeat for at least 2 cycles = 18 periods. On occasion it will repeat for more than 5 cycles (5 waves) but then it will shift. The trader can learn two valuable lessons from this phenomenon. First, once the cycle has changed begin to look for the new nominal cycle. Second, once a nominal cycle has been identified keep using it until it stops working. That certainly sounds simple enough.

The study of cycles can be improved by using the principles of rational proportion. If you think of a price chart on any stock or commodity as nothing more than a road map, then all you need to do is connect the dots to get to the destination. The following diagram is an oversimplification of what I'm trying to convey.

If the trader (analyst) will use the principle of ratio and proportion it can leave valuable clues to the validity of a cycle. Reminder--- we are dealing with probabilities only. Nothing is written as absolute law.

"Take care of your losses and your profits will take care of themselves."

---Amos Hostetter
Commodity Corp.

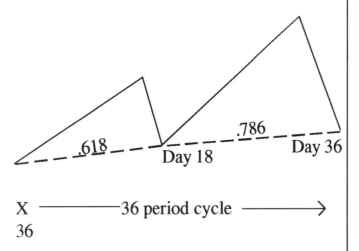

X ⎯⎯⎯⎯ 36 period cycle ⎯⎯⎯→
36

Fibonacci Trading Card:

My method of trading while on the floor of the CME was actually quite simple. Each night I would prepare the next day's trading from my apartment at McClurg Court. I kept daily charts on about 20 commodities and intraday charts on all major CME futures contracts. While on the floor, I would still trade Silver and Soybeans regularly, but the bulk of trading was in T-Bills and Gold. Later, it would be in the S&P 500 pit, but that didn't start trading until April of 1982. Because I did not like to enter the pits to trade for myself, I would physically hand the pit broker my order. I kept a swing chart on a trading card in my jacket. This is what it would look like:

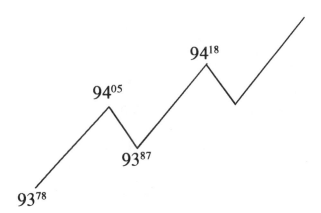

As prices would approach my buying or selling points I would watch the "runners" bringing orders into the pit from their respective commission houses. During a sharp rally or sell-off, this activity is really easy to see. As the activity slackened I moved to the pit and took the opposite side (sell rallies --buy dips). I used a trading card with all of the Fibonacci numbers and the .618 and 1.618 relationships. As mentioned earlier, I did not know the importance of the square roots of these numbers until 1989. The following 2 pages are a replica of the trading card I carried. I've included a card with the .786 and 1.27 relationships for your convenience. I still use these cards to this day, but now they are much larger and are placed on wooden frames hanging over my desk.

Notice the price of the S&P in the chart. That is the price it was trading at in 1982-83. The nearby futures would routinely trade at a discount to the cash S&P.

Fibonacci Trading Card					.786/1.27
04 05 06	17 21 27	29 37 47	42 53 67	54 69 88	67 85 108
05 06 08	17 22 28	30 38 48	42 54 69	55 70 89	68 86 109
06 07 09	18 23 29	31 39 50	43 55 70	56 71 90	68 87 110
06 08 10	19 24 30	31 40 51	44 56 71	57 72 91	69 88 112
07 09 11	20 25 32	32 41 52	45 57 72	57 73 93	70 89 113
08 10 13	20 26 33	33 42 53	46 58 74	58 74 94	71 90 114
09 11 14	21 27 34	34 43 55	46 59 75	59 75 95	72 91 116
09 12 15	22 28 36	35 44 56	47 60 76	60 76 97	72 92 117
10 13 17	23 29 37	35 45 57	48 61 77	61 77 98	73 93 118
11 14 18	24 30 38	36 46 58	49 62 79	61 78 99	74 94 119
12 15 19	24 31 39	37 47 60	50 63 80	62 79 100	75 95 121
13 16 20	25 32 41	38 48 61	50 64 81	63 80 102	76 96 122
13 17 22	26 33 42	39 49 62	51 65 83	64 81 103	76 97 123
14 18 23	27 34 43	39 50 64	52 66 84	64 82 104	77 98 124
15 19 24	28 35 44	40 51 65	53 67 85	65 83 105	78 99 126
16 20 25	28 36 46	41 52 66	53 68 86	66 84 107	

Example: 28 **36** 46   Multiply   36 x .786 = 28   36 x 1.27 = 46

Fibonacci Trading Card .618/1.618

$_{10}06_{04}$	$_{34}21_{13}$	$_{60}37_{23}$	$_{84}52_{32}$	$_{110}68_{42}$	$_{136}84_{52}$
$_{11}07_{04}$	$_{36}22_{14}$	$_{61}38_{23}$	$_{86}53_{33}$	$_{112}69_{43}$	$_{138}85_{53}$
$_{13}08_{05}$	$_{37}23_{14}$	$_{63}39_{24}$	$_{87}54_{33}$	$_{113}70_{43}$	$_{139}86_{53}$
$_{15}09_{06}$	$_{39}24_{15}$	$_{65}40_{25}$	$_{89}55_{34}$	$_{115}71_{44}$	$_{141}87_{54}$
$_{16}10_{06}$	$_{40}25_{15}$	$_{66}41_{25}$	$_{91}56_{35}$	$_{116}72_{44}$	$_{142}88_{54}$
$_{18}11_{07}$	$_{42}26_{16}$	$_{68}42_{26}$	$_{92}57_{35}$	$_{118}73_{45}$	$_{144}89_{55}$
$_{19}12_{07}$	$_{44}27_{17}$	$_{70}43_{27}$	$_{94}58_{36}$	$_{120}74_{46}$	$_{146}90_{56}$
$_{21}13_{08}$	$_{45}28_{17}$	$_{71}44_{27}$	$_{95}59_{36}$	$_{121}75_{46}$	$_{147}91_{56}$
$_{23}14_{09}$	$_{47}29_{18}$	$_{73}45_{28}$	$_{97}60_{37}$	$_{123}76_{47}$	$_{149}92_{57}$
$_{24}15_{09}$	$_{49}30_{19}$	$_{74}46_{28}$	$_{99}61_{38}$	$_{125}77_{48}$	$_{150}93_{57}$
$_{26}16_{10}$	$_{50}31_{19}$	$_{76}47_{29}$	$_{101}62_{38}$	$_{126}78_{48}$	$_{152}94_{58}$
$_{28}17_{11}$	$_{52}32_{20}$	$_{78}48_{30}$	$_{102}63_{39}$	$_{128}79_{49}$	$_{154}95_{59}$
$_{29}18_{11}$	$_{53}33_{20}$	$_{79}49_{30}$	$_{104}64_{40}$	$_{129}80_{49}$	$_{155}96_{59}$
$_{31}19_{12}$	$_{55}34_{21}$	$_{81}50_{31}$	$_{105}65_{40}$	$_{131}81_{50}$	$_{157}97_{60}$
$_{32}20_{12}$	$_{56}35_{21}$	$_{83}51_{32}$	$_{107}66_{41}$	$_{133}82_{51}$	$_{159}98_{61}$
	$_{58}36_{22}$		$_{108}67_{41}$	$_{134}83_{51}$	$_{160}99_{6}$

Example: 35_{21} Multiply $36 \times .618 = 21$ Add $21 + 35 = 56$ (1.618 of 35)

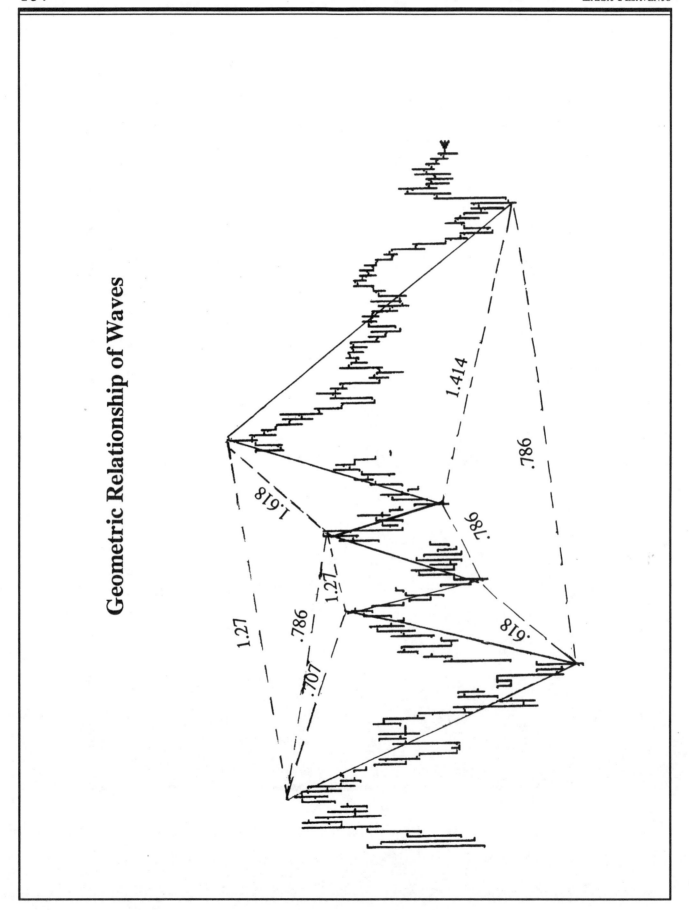

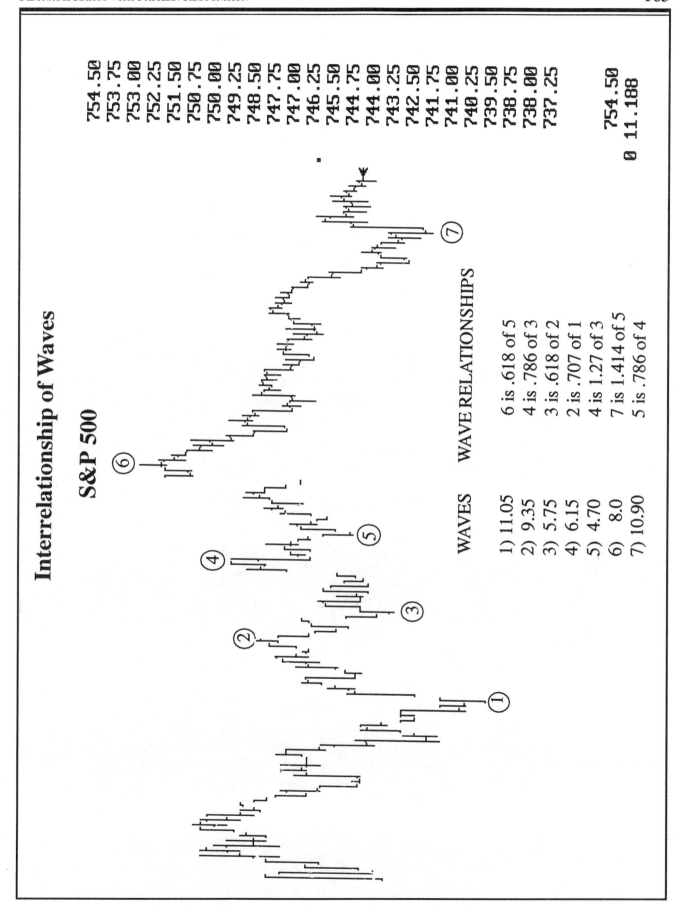

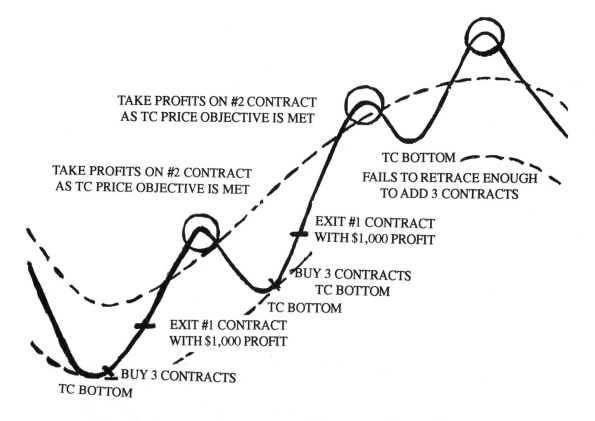

Controlled Risk Money Management

30,000 X 10% = 3,000	$ Risk	% Risk
#1 Money Contract	1,000	3 1/3%
#2 Trading Contract	1,000	3 1/3%
#3 Long Term Contract	1,000	3 1/3%

TAKE PROFITS ON BOTH #3 CONTRACTS AS LONG TERM PRICE OBJECTIVES ARE MET

TAKE PROFITS ON #2 CONTRACT AS TC PRICE OBJECTIVE IS MET

TAKE PROFITS ON #2 CONTRACT AS TC PRICE OBJECTIVE IS MET

TC BOTTOM FAILS TO RETRACE ENOUGH TO ADD 3 CONTRACTS

EXIT #1 CONTRACT WITH $1,000 PROFIT

BUY 3 CONTRACTS TC BOTTOM

TC BOTTOM

EXIT #1 CONTRACT WITH $1,000 PROFIT

BUY 3 CONTRACTS

TC BOTTOM

This chart is courtesy of Walter Bressert, PO Box 8268, Indian River Shores, Florida, 32963-1014. Mr. Bressert is a pioneer in cycle research and a director of the Foundation for the Study of Cycles. The chart is presented to alert our readers to the importance of risk control in trading all markets.

APPENDIX VI
SOME MORE PRACTICAL TIPS
MONEY MANAGEMENT

"Lose your opinion instead of your money"
---Paul Tudor Jones

I. Money management in risk speculation should be kept simple. Here are some "unbreakable rules" and some "guidelines."

    A. Unbreakable Rules
        1. Never add to a losing position.
        2. Never risk *more than 10 percent* of your trading capital on any one trade.
        3. Always have a protective stop in the market.
        4. If you don't have a profit in three days, exit the trade.

    B. Guidelines
        1. Never close a trade without a reason.
        2. Take responsibility for your trades.
        3. Markets that have higher lows are in uptrends. Markets that have lower highs are in downtrends.
        4. Always do your analysis prior to the market open.

II. Ask these questions before closing a position.
    A. Does the position show a loss?
    B. Has it reached the price objective?
    C. Are you convinced your opinion is wrong?

If the answer to all three of these questions is *NO*, then you must hold your position. If the answer to any one of the three is a YES, then you *may* close the trade if you wish.

III. Observations

    A. Calculate your trading capital and multiply by three percent. This will give you the amount of loss you can take on any trade. Example: $10,000 x 3% = $300. You should only risk $300 on the trade.
    B. As your account grows you must still use the three percent guideline, but you can trade more contracts.
    C. If you are able to trade multiple contracts you should consider using a "trailing" stop on one of the positions. This stems from the ability of the system to enter at major turning points in the market.
    D. The trader must always protect himself from his own fallibility. Stops are placed for protection against yourself. *"Markets are seldom wrong; men often are!"* –Roy Longstreet

"Life is a do-it yourself project."

IV. Recommended reading
    A. *Reminiscences of a Stock Operator,* Edwin Lefevre
    B. *The Disciplined Trader,* Mark Douglass
    C. *The Warrior Athlete,* Dan Millman
    D. *The Art of War,* Sun Tsu
    E. *The Psychology of Winning,* Dennis Waitley

The Volatility Stop Entry Technique

The Volatility Stop calculates the volatility by using the average range of the price bar. It is calculated by multiplying the average range by a constant. The value is added to the lowest close when short, and subtracted from the highest high when long:

Range = (Range x (N - 1) + High - Low / N)
Short = Lowest Close + Range x C
Long   = Highest Close - Range x C

My experience is to use the Volatility Stop in strongly trending markets. It is an excellent entry technique and in most instances will be superior to valid trend line breaks, or channel breakouts. The reverse stop also acts to quantify risk as it relates to volatility. The constants should be kept between 2.5 and 4.0.

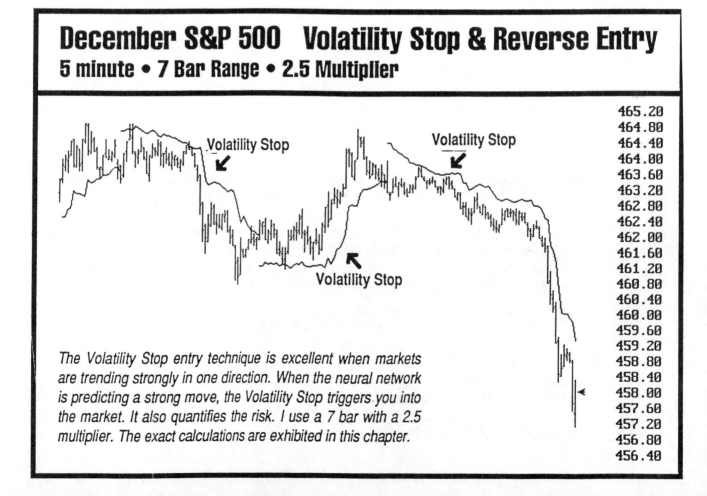

DANGER SIGNALS!

Markets are seldom wrong! There is one fact that is always present in the markets: If prices go up there are more buyers; if prices go down there are more sellers! Here are a few technical indicators that suggest a market may be changing character:

A. Gaps

A big price gap on a chart is indicative of a change in sentiment and deserves attention. Use the *Shapiro Iteration* (wait one bar) before acting.

B. Wide Range

When price ranges become abnormally wide then price objectives are more likely to be exceeded (1.618). You should know the average daily range of the commodity you are trading.

C. Tail Close

Markets that close at the extreme top or bottom are indicating strength or weakness. Look for several days of tail closes in the same direction.

"Take care of your losses and the profits will take of themselves."
----Amos Hostetter
Commodity Corporation (circa 1967)

RULES OF JESSE LIVERMORE
Excerpted from *Reminscences of a Stock Operator*
by Edwin LeFevre

1. Of all the speculative blunders, there are few greater than trying to average a losing game.

2. Always sell what shows you a loss and keep what shows you a profit.

3. You cannot try to force the market into giving you something it does not have to give.

4. The courage in a specualtor is merely the confidence to act on the decision of his mind.

5. A loss never bothers me after I take it. I forget it overnight. But being wrong--not taking the loss--that is what does the damage to the pocketbook and to the soul.

6. The man who is right always has two forces working in his favor--basic conditions and the men who are wrong.

7. The trend is evident to a man who has an open mind and reasonably clear sight. It is never wise for a speculator to fit his facts to his theories.

8. In a narrow market when price moves within a narrow range, the thing to do is watch the market, read the tape to determine the limits of prices, and make up your mind that you will not take an interest until the price breaks through the limit in either direction.

9. You watch the market with one objective: to determine the direction or price tendency. Price like everything else, move along the line of least resistance.

10. In the long run commodtiy prices are governed but by one law---the economic law of suppl and demand.

11. It costs me millions to learn that a dangerous enemy to a trader is his susceptibility to the urging of a magnetic personality combined with a brilliant mind.

12. Have a profit---forget it! Have a loss, forget it even quicker!

13. It never was my thinking that made the big money for me. It was always my sitting, my sittin tight.

14. There is only one side to the stock market and it is not the bull side or the bear side, but the right side.

HE WHO KNOWS NOT
WHAT HE RISKS...
RISKS ALL!

There are three rules you need to develop in order to trade successfully:

1. Build a foundation of trust in yourself so that you will act in your own best interests---without hesitation.

2. Follow a set of steps that will build confidence and a belief in your own consistency. This includes learning to not give your money away.

3. Execute your trades flawlessly when a signal is given. Ask yourself these three questions:

    a) Is it an identifiable pattern?
    b) Are the sacred ratios present?
    c) Can I afford to take the risk?

If the answer to these three questions is 'yes!' then you should take the trade.

Keep in mind these important factors:

- Money management always takes precedent over any trading methodology. You must never expose yourself to unlimited risk. Stops are placed for protection against yourself.

- Never get into a trade where the risk is unknown.

- The mistake is not **being** wrong; the mistake is in **staying** wrong!

- Fear causes us to narrow our focus of attention and distorts our perception of the environment.

- Self-discipline is the ability of maintaining your focus of attention when all the things in the environment are in conflict.

- Never let the market save you---you must save Yourself. Use stops!

- We deal in probabilities! The market is always greater than anything we can ever anticipate. No methodology of trading can tell you what is going to happen next. Profits come from string of trades and not from one particular trade.

- Take care of hour losses and the profits will take care of themselves! Release yourself from being wrong or the fear of losing money. Trading is not a game of right or wrong, it is the process of making money.

- Be rigid in your rules and flexible with your observations.

APPENDIX VII
JANUARY 2, 1997

This day will end the writing of this book. It is included because of its wild swings. The Dow Jones dropped more than 100 points during the day and then recovered all of the loss in the last 25 minutes. The S&P 500 dropped 16 points, rallied 9 points, dropped 9 points and then closed up on the day. Traders should keep in mind that the volatility of the stock market has been very mild since 1990. It might behoove the trader to prepare for increased volatility in the next few years.

Fibonacci Ratios with Pattern Recognition

173

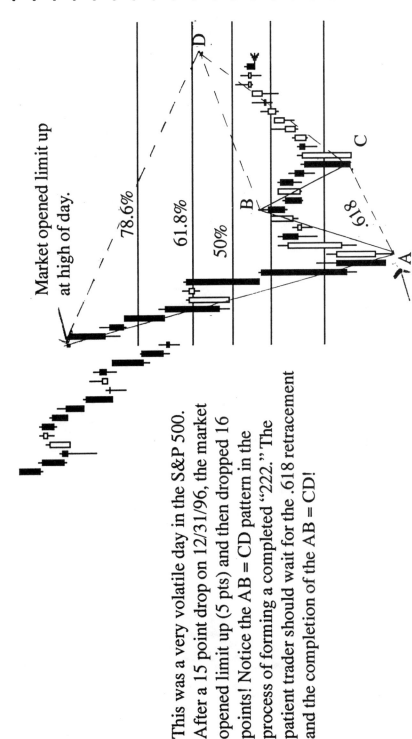

January 2nd, 1997
March S&P 500 (5 min)
Formation of the Gartley "222" Pattern

This was a very volatile day in the S&P 500. After a 15 point drop on 12/31/96, the market opened limit up (5 pts) and then dropped 16 points! Notice the AB = CD pattern in the process of forming a completed "222." The patient trader should wait for the .618 retracement and the completion of the AB = CD!

Market opened limit up at high of day.

Point A is an exact .786 retracement on the daily charts.

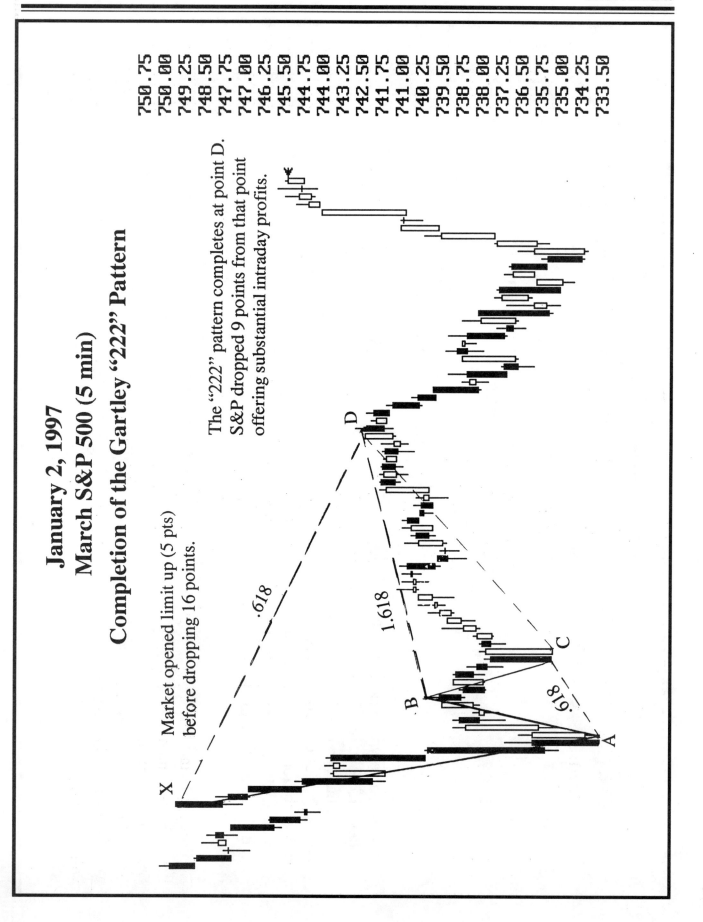

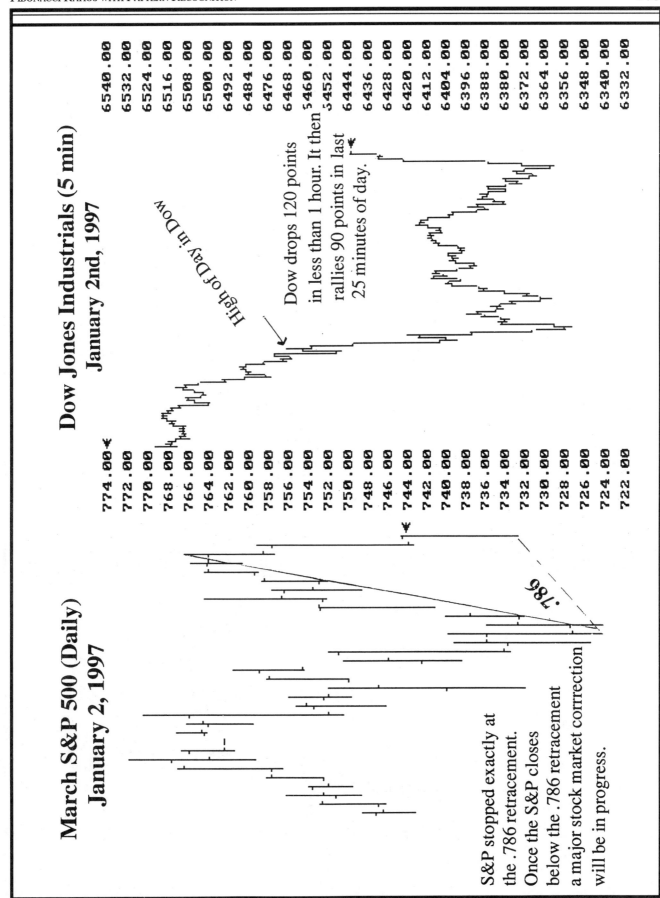

ADDITIONAL Reading

Art of War. Sun Tsu.

Astro Cycles in Speculative Markets. Jensen, L. (Lambert-Gann Publishing).

Astro-Cycles: The Trader's Viewpoint. Pesavento, Larry. (AstroCycles, 1988).

Astro-Economic Interpretation. Jensen, L. (Lambert-Gann Publishing).

Business Cycles Versus Planetary Movements. Langham, J.M. (Maghnal).

Capital Ideas: The Improbable Origins of Modern Wall Street. Bernstein, Peter. (New York Free Press, 1992).

Chaos and Order in the Capital Markets. Peters, Edgar. (John Wiley & Sons, 1991).

Commodity Futures Trading with Point and Figure. Maxwell, Joseph.

Cycles-The Science of Prediction. Daiken, Dewey. (Foundation Study of Cycles).

Cyclical Market Forecasting: Stocks and Grains. Langham, J.M. (Maghnal).

Divine Proportion. Huntley. (Dover Press).

Economic Cycles: Their Law and Course. Moore, H. (Macmillan).

Elliott Wave Principle. Prechter Robert. (New Classics Library).

Extraordinary Popular Delusions and the Madness of Crowds. Mackay, Chuck.

ADDITIONAL Reading

Fibonacci Applications and Strategies for Traders. Fischer, Robert.

Forecasting Financial Markets: The Truth Behind Technical Analysis. Plummer, Tony. (Kogan Page Ltd., London, 1990).

Forecasting Prices. Butaney, T.G. (Pearl Printing).

Geometry of Markets. Gilmore, Bryce T. (Bryce Gilmore & Assoc., Pty Ltd., Melbourne, Australia, 1989).

Geometry of Markets II. Gilmore, Bryce T. (Bryce Gilmore & Assoc., Pty Ltd., Melbourne, Australia, 1993).

Geometry of Stock Market Profits. Pesavento, Larry. (Trader's Press, Inc., 1996).

Harmonic Vibrations. Pesavento, Larry. (Trader's Press, Inc. 1996).

Investing for Profit with Torque Analysis of Stock Market Cycles. Garrett, W. ((Ruff Pub. 508-448-6739)

Market Wizards: Interviews with Top Traders. Schwager, Jack D. (Simon & Schuster, 1989).

Mastering Elliott Wave. Neely, Glenn.

Mathematics of Money Management. Vince, Ralph.

Planetary Effects on Stock Market Prices. Langham, J.M. (Maghnal).

Planetary Harmonics of Speculative Markets. Pesavento Larry. (Astro-Cycles, 1990).

Profit Magic of Stock Transactions Timing. Hurst, J. (Prentice

ADDITIONAL Reading

Rocky Mountain Financial Workbook. Foster, W. (Box 1093, Reseda, CA 91355).

Secret Teaching of All Ages. Hall, M.P.(Philosophical Society of Los Angeles).

Stock and Commodity Trader's Handbook of Trend Determinators. Bayer, George. (Out of Print.)

Stock Market Prediction. Bradley. (Llewellyn Publishing).

Technical Analysis of the Futures Markets. Murphy, John

Technical Analysis of Stock Trends. Edwards and Magee

The Dimensions of Paradise: The Proportions and Symbolic Numbers of Ancient Cosmology. Mitchell, John. (Harper & Row, 1988)

The Disciplined Trader: Developing Winning Attitudes. Douglass, Mark (New York Institute of Finance, 1990)

The Kabala of Numbers Sepherial (Newcastle).

The Magic Word. Gann, W.D. (Lambert-Gann Publishing).

The Major Works of R.N. Elliott. (New Classics Library).

The Outer Game of Trading. Koppel, Robert and Abell, Howard. (Proteus Publishing, 1974).

The Secret of the Ages. Collier, Robert.

Time Factors in the Stock Market. Bayer, George. (Out of print.)

Tunnel Through the Air. Gann, W. D (Lambert-Gann Publishing).

MARKET ART!

Market-related art is available through
TRADERS PRESS.

If interested in full details, please contact:

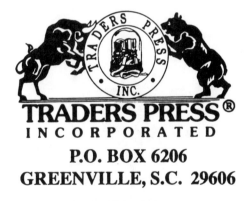

TRADERS PRESS®
INCORPORATED
**P.O. BOX 6206
GREENVILLE, S.C. 29606**

*Books and Gifts
for Investors and Traders*

1-800-927-8222   FAX 864-298-0221
Tradersprs@aol.com

• TECHNICAL ANALYSIS • OPTIONS • TRADING PSYCHOLOGY & DISCIPLINE • SPREAD TRADING • ELLIOTT WAVE • W.D. GANN • INTRADAY TRADING • TRADING STRATEGIES

FREE TRADERS CATALOG

• FIBONACCI • FLOOR TRADING • 31 FREE BOOKS (WITH ADDITIONAL PURCHASE) • MONEY MANAGEMENT • MUTUAL FUNDS • SHORT SELLING / BEAR MARKETS • STOCK INDEX TRADING • SYSTEMS AND METHODS • MANY OTHER TOPICS •

TRADERS PRESS, INC. publishes a 72-page catalog which lists and describes hundreds of books, tapes, courses and gifts of interest to stock, options, and futures traders.
(Regular price $5)

Get your FREE copy by writing, calling or faxing
TRADERS PRESS, INC.

Edward D. Dobson
TRADERS PRESS, INC.®
P.O. BOX 6206
GREENVILLE, SC 29606

Serving traders since 1975

TRADERS PRESS®
INCORPORATED

800-927-8222
864-298-0222
FAX: 864-298-0221
Tradersprs@aol.com